21世纪应用型人才培养规划教材

实用商务英语口语

Spoken English for Business Communication

主　编　刘　娟　张　冰
副主编　石东华

北京理工大学出版社
BEIJING INSTITUTE OF TECHNOLOGY PRESS

版权专有　侵权必究

图书在版编目（CIP）数据

实用商务英语口语/刘娟，张冰主编．—北京：北京理工大学出版社，2015.1（2018.2重印）

ISBN 978－7－5682－0139－1

Ⅰ.①实…　Ⅱ.①刘…②张…　Ⅲ.①商务－英语－口语－高等学校－教材　Ⅳ.①H319.9

中国版本图书馆 CIP 数据核字（2015）第 005192 号

出版发行 /北京理工大学出版社有限责任公司
社　　址 /北京市海淀区中关村南大街 5 号
邮　　编 /100081
电　　话 /（010）68914775（总编室）
　　　　　82562903（教材售后服务热线）
　　　　　68948351（其他图书服务热线）
网　　址 /http：//www.bitpress.com.cn
经　　销 /全国各地新华书店
印　　刷 /虎彩印艺股份有限公司
开　　本 /710 毫米×1000 毫米　1/16
印　　张 /9.25　　　　　　　　　　　　　　　责任编辑 /武丽娟
字　　数 /199 千字　　　　　　　　　　　　　 文案编辑 /武丽娟
版　　次 /2015 年 1 月第 1 版　2018 年 2 月第 3 次印刷　责任校对 /周瑞红
定　　价 /23.00 元　　　　　　　　　　　　　　责任印制 /马振武

图书出现印装质量问题，请拨打售后服务热线，本社负责调换

  本教材属于"大学英语"课程的辅助教材。依据英语课程及专业需求教学的基本理念，教材在内容的选择上，从提高学生素质和加强应用的角度选材，适当取舍，来满足此类专业未来岗位的普遍需求。针对不同专业的学生特点及专业课程英语的需求，教材增加了口语的应用内容，构成不同专业的英语课程体系。实施单元式、互动的、多层次的教学，以满足职业岗位群的需求。突出口语教学，分专业融入不同口语实践教材，形成一套与主教材并行的商务、金融类口语教学内容，以强化英语的口语交际的应用，体现高职英语的应用价值。

  本教材各章节设以下部分：相关知识介绍、情景对话、重点词汇及句式以及任务安排。话题包括各种商务及金融活动：商务类内容涵盖营销策略、企业文化、市场竞争、风险投资、客户服务等各个方面；金融类内容包括柜台业务，如开立账户、存款、取款、外汇交易、信用证、电子银行等方面。话题力求新颖，模拟真实场景再现，且有助于学生做好初到职场的英语沟通技能上的铺垫和心理上的准备，充分体现实用、够用的原则。在相关知识介绍环节，可使学生们初步接触相关专业知识，将专业课程与英语内容有机结合。情景对话使学生们实际操作相应场景的英文交际，切实锻炼提高学生的口语能力以及相关场景的交流及礼仪礼节。重点词汇及句式可进一步加强和巩固学生们对本章里所学知识的概括和整理；通过对词汇和句式的掌握，学生可在相应场景口语交流中增强知识储备，真正做到活学活用，学为所用。任务安排部分则通过任务驱动方法检验学生们对本章内知识的掌握，在实战演练阶段互相学习，提高自己所学专业知识的口语表达能力。背景知识介绍部分提供给学生们与本单元话题相关的趣味知识，激发他们的想象力及其对更广泛专业知识的兴趣。

本教材根据教育部最新发布的高职高专院校大学英语课程培养目标和要求编写而成，适合作为高职高专院校的国际商务、物流管理、报关及国际货运代理、金融、连锁、会电等专业的教科书或补充材料。在编写过程中，编者参考了大量的同类教材和商业银行网站资料，在此表示衷心的感谢。

现代社会是一个信息化高度发展的时代，编者虽然斟酌反复，几易其稿，力求与时俱进，但由于时间仓促，书中的不足和疏忽之处在所难免，敬请广大读者批评指正。

目 录 contents

第一部分　商务篇 1
- Unit 1　Entertaining Business Clients 3
- Unit 2　Establishing Business Relations 11
- Unit 3　Inquiry and Offer 19
- Unit 4　Packing and Insurance 27
- Unit 5　Shipment and Payment 36
- Unit 6　Seeing off Business Clients 45
- Appendix 58

第二部分　金融篇 71
- Unit 1　Daily Reception 73
- Unit 2　Deposit and Withdrawal 81
- Unit 3　Remittance 89
- Unit 4　Loans and Credit Cards 97
- Unit 5　E-banking 105
- Appendix 114

参考文献 142

第一部分

商 务 篇

Unit 1 Entertaining Business Clients

 Expected Goals

1. When dealing with international trade, you should get familiar with the process of making appointments, picking up guests at the airport, and inviting them to business dinners.
2. Skillfully apply useful expressions related to entertaining foreign guests to daily conversations.

Lead-in

The ability to entertain clients is one of the essential skills to be equipped with for any company. The way you behave not only represents your corporate culture, but also constitutes a part of the first impression on your clients. If you impress your clients positively, it means repeat business and other perks down the road.

The connection between your company and potential customers begins with telephone appointment and ends up with having a formal meal. The trick to entertaining clients is to find out what they enjoy doing and make sure that they have a good time while in your company. Therefore, you are supposed to rack your brain over a series of activities, such as playing tennis, a sightseeing tour, a concert performance, or a business banquet. These warming-up activities are not necessarily aimed at concluding a deal, but you may find the distance between the two sides is much narrower than the beginning. In view of this, much preparation must be made about understanding the client's educational background, cultural difference and personal preference beforehand.

 Situational Dialogues

Dialogue One Making an Appointment

A—Joan, Assistant of Mr. Lee   B—Mr. King

(Ringing)

A: Hello. This is Sales Department. Can I help you?

B: Hello. This is King. I'm calling to make an appointment with your director, Mr. Lee, about your newly launched product.

A: Yes. Wait a moment. Let me check Mr. Lee's agenda. Oh, he is fully occupied this week. How about next week?

B: Um…I'm afraid not. You know I just arrived in Shanghai yesterday, and I have to go back to New York next Monday. It's really urgent for us to discuss the details of the cooperation in person. So could you try to arrange it for sometime later this week?

A: Let me see what I can do. Mr. Lee intends to attend a banquet on Friday afternoon which may last two hours. Is that convenient for you on Friday?

B: It couldn't be better. What time exactly?

A: How about 4 p.m. at the conference room?

B: Great, that's settled.

A: OK. Looking forward to seeing you then.

B: Many thanks. I'll be there on time.

Notes：

1. "appointment"与"date"的意思都是"约会"，但是含义不同。"appointment"常用于商务会谈，是比较正式的预约；而"date"仅指一般性的约会。比如：

He has an appointment with the doctor this afternoon. 今天下午他和医生有个约会。He dated his girlfriend on Sunday. 他和他的女朋友在周日有约会。

2. launch a product 产品上市

3. agenda 日程

4. banquet 比 dinner 更正式，用于商务社交场合，代指盛大的晚宴。

5. It couldn't be better. 那再好不过了。

Dialogue Two Meeting Guests at the Airport

A—Joan, Assistant of Mr. Lee   B—Mr. King

A: Excuse me. Are you Mr. King from Shanghai?

B: That's it. How do you do?

A: How do you do, Mr. King. Welcome to Tianjin. I'm the assistant of Mr. Lee, Joan. Mr. Lee was unexpectedly tied up today. He's sorry he can't come over to meet you personally.

B: That's OK. It's very kind of you to have come.

A: There's a car waiting for you just outside the door. Right this way, please. How was your flight?

B: Not bad. There was a dense fog here, so the flight was delayed some time.

A: Oh, you must be very tired. Let me help you with the luggage.

B: No, thanks. I can manage it.

A: We'll reach Tianjin Hotel in another ten minutes. And I've reserved a quiet single room for you there so that you can have a good rest.

B: Oh, you are so thoughtful.

A: If it's convenient for you, Mr. Lee would like to invite you to dinner in honor of you tonight.

B: Thank you, I will. When and where will the dinner be?

A: At six o'clock in the International Hotel. We'll pick you up this afternoon. Besides, if you care for visiting, we'll arrange some sightseeing for you.

B: Oh, that's nice. Thanks for arranging all of this.

Notes:

1. be tied up 繁忙，抽不开身(同样的表达还有：be occupied / be fully booked / be not available)

2. dense fog 浓雾

3. luggage 行李(美国一般用 baggage，均为不可数名词，例如：two pieces / articles of luggage 两件行李)

4. single-room 单人房；double-room 双人房

5. in honor of sb. 为了向……表示敬意

6. pick sb. up 用汽车搭载某人或接某人，如：I'll pick you up at seven o'clock. 我将在七点钟开车来接你。

7. sightseeing *n.* 观光

Dialogue Three　Holding Business Dinner

A—Mr. Lee　　B—Mr. King

A：We are happy you are here today, Mr. King. Welcome to Tianjin.

B：Nice to meet you, Mr. Lee. I'm grateful for you to prepare such a splendid dinner especially for me.

A：It's my honor. I know how busy you are. On behalf of my company, may I propose a toast to you? Thanks for your attention to our products.

B：Cheers! In fact, I've heard a lot about your company. It enjoys a high reputation abroad.

A：Oh, it's flattered. I'm eager to have a further communication with you over the next few days.

B：So am I. To a long friendship, cheers!

（Three hours later…）

B：All good things come to an end, as they say. So if you don't mind, I've got to run.

A：Oh, it's a pity that you have to leave so early.

B：Indeed, the schedule for me is tight every day. See you tomorrow morning when I visit your factory. Thanks again for your wonderful meal. And I hope to have a chance to repay your hospitality some day.

A：I'm glad you enjoy it. See you then.

Notes：

1. splendid dinner 丰盛的晚餐

2. It's my honor. 荣幸之至。

3. on behalf of sb. 代表某人

4. propose a toast to sb. 向某人敬酒；干杯

5. It's flattered. 您过奖了。

6. All good things come to an end. 天下无不散之筵席。

7. hospitality 热情好客，盛情款待

Useful Patterns

1. Could I make an appointment with your Marketing Manager on Friday?
   本周五能预约贵公司的市场营销部经理吗？

2. Let me check his diary and see if I can arrange it for you. Hold on, please...Mr. King might be free on Tuesday.
   我先看看日程表再决定能否为您安排约见。请等一下，金先生周二可能有空。

3. I'm afraid I won't be available tomorrow morning. I wonder if you could spare some time next week.
   恐怕明早我没有时间。下周您看能抽出时间见面吗？

4. You must be Mr. King from the United States? I'm Joan, the secretary of Grand Corporation.
   您一定是美国的金先生吧？我是乔安，格兰德公司的秘书。

5. Let's go and get you checked into the hotel and have a good rest.
   我们先去办理酒店入住手续吧，您可以在那里好好休息。

6. This trip was awfully long and a bit turbulent.
   飞行时间过长而且气流有些颠簸。

7. I wonder if you have had any plans tonight.
   不知道您今晚有没有什么安排？

8. I'd like to hold a banquet in your honor. What about six o'clock at

Hongqi Restaurant to have a typical Chinese food?
我想设宴为您接风洗尘,今晚六点在红旗饭店吃传统中餐如何？

9. Here's an invitation card for you.
这是给您的请柬。

10. I'm grateful to you for giving me such an unforgettable evening.
很感激您让我度过了一个难忘的夜晚。

11. Well, to your health and success in business, cheers!
来,祝你身体健康,生意兴隆,干杯!

Role-playing

1. Mr. Black is a representative of ABC Textile Products Company from Canada, which has close business connections with your company. You, assistant of PR Department, are assigned to pick him up at the airport and arrange a proper sightseeing for him. Now make up a dialogue.

2. Your company found a potential buyer through some other channel, but you had no correspondence with him before. In this case the buyer will hint that he is very busy and has no time to meet you. So please try to persuade the buyer to give you a chance to show him your products.

文化知更多

外国客户来公司参观前应先熟悉公司介绍和产品资料,备好文件和样品。尽量亲自去接机,让客户看到你的诚心。接机的时候可以多向对方介绍本地的情况、特色旅游的景点、美食以及最近的天气状况,并确认其在中国的行程安排。如能抽出时间,带客人参观一下城市美丽的风景或名胜,让他们加深印象。准备一些中国特色的礼物在离别时送给客户,如茶具、茶叶等。当然,最重要的是你对于公司和产品的介绍,要让客户相信你们公司有能力生产出质量好的产品；如果双方在价格上也能谈得拢，那就恭喜你了。

TIPS：

a. 外国人通常有着很强的时间观念，无论什么情况一定不要迟到，最好提前15分钟。

b. 出于商务原因见面时，互递名片已经成为一种礼节，建议不要把名片直接放在口袋里，而是要准备一个名片盒。

c. 帮外国人预订酒店时，如果不止一人，一定要尽量安排单人房间，外国人的私密感很重要！

Unit 2 Establishing Business Relations

 Expected Goals

1. Get familiar with the common oral expressions on establishing business relations with foreign guests.
2. Learn the basic business skills and etiquettes when dealing with foreign trade.

 Lead-in

No customer, no business. Business relations are very important for operation and expansion of companies. Establishing good business relations is the starting point as well as ultimate goal for negotiations. Merchants may be approached through the following channels such as introduction from banks, business connections, Chamber of Commerce, Commercial Counselor's Office, etc. Then companies may communicate with each other by mutual visits, attendance at trade fairs and exhibitions held at home and abroad. Usually a company invites its customers to visit the products or the company itself takes ways to attract potential customers, which is an effective way to help establish business relations.

Situational Dialogues

Dialogue One Show Around the Factory

A—Mr. Lee   B—Mr. King

A: Good morning, Mr. King, Welcome to visit our factory.

B: Morning, Mr. Lee. Pleased to see you again.

A: I'm here to give you a tour around the plant. Please feel free to ask questions at any point during our tour.

B: Yes, I will. Thanks. By the way, how many employees does your factory have?

A: About 600 employees. We are running on three shifts. This way, please. Look, this is our office block. All the administrative departments are here.

B: Oh, what are they?

A: Sales, Accounting, Personnel, Market Research and so on.

B: What's that building opposite us?

A: That's the warehouse which is used to store our goods. We keep a stock of the best-sellers in order to meet the urgent need from stock.

B: Oh, I see. What are those people doing over there?

A: They are checking for quality. We established the strict QC standards, and we have followed it for about ten years with good results.

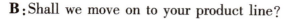

B：Shall we move on to your product line?

A：Of course. Our modern equipment guarantees the high quality of our products and the production speed as well.

…

A：Mr. King, what's your overall impression of our factory?

B：Very impressive. I hope to cooperate with you in the future.

A：Great. Would you like to discuss a few details over lunch?

B：Good idea.

Notes：

1. on three shifts 三班制
2. office block 办公楼
3. administrative department 行政部门
4. warehouse 仓库
5. best-seller 畅销品
6. guarantee 保证

Dialogue Two   Visit the Showroom

A—Mr. Lee   B—Mr. King

A：Mr. King, here's our showroom.

B：Oh, you've got a wide range of sample foodstuffs here.

A：Yes, we are exporting a variety of foodstuffs to many countries. And they enjoy excellent reputation. By the way, what items are you interested in?

B：I'm interested in biscuit. Could you show me some samples?

A：Yes. Follow me. Our biscuit has various tastes such as milk biscuit, honey biscuit, soda biscuit, etc. There are altogether 15 tastes.

B：Could I have a try, Mr. Lee?

A：Of course. We have small packages of 50 grams for each taste. You

13

can even take some back to taste slowly.

B: Thanks for your consideration. By the way, do you have any catalogue or price list for my reference?

A: Here you are. Our biscuits are sold well at home and abroad, and many customers speak highly of their tastes and qualities.

B: Really? I also heard of your products from one of my connections. No wonder you are so confident. More importantly, how about your food safety?

A: Please rest assured. You know, the governmental restrictions have been getting tighter, so our foodstuffs are guaranteed to conform to WHO standards.

B: That's great. Well, I wonder if your price is competitive.

A: The biscuits have been sold in your country for 5 years. If you're determined to import from us, in order to encourage business, I'll allow you a large discount.

B: Thanks again. I'll contact you for details as soon as possible.

A: My pleasure. Looking forward to your early reply.

Notes:

1. showroom 展室
2. enjoy excellent reputation 享有盛誉
3. catalogue 产品目录
4. price list 价格单
5. for one's reference 供某人参考
6. at home and abroad 国内外
7. rest assured 请放心
8. WHO(全称为 World Health Organization.) 世界卫生组织
9. discount 折扣

Dialogue Three　　Enter into Business Relations

A—Mr. King　　B—Mr. Lee

A: Mr. Lee, I've gone over the catalogue and the pamphlets of your company. Now I've a feeling that we can do a lot of trade in this line.

B: Great, your desire coincides with ours, Mr. King.

A: What's your products' competitive edge?

B: You have probably noticed that our products have met with great favor overseas and are always in great demand. Besides, the prices are competitive.

A: We need your detailed explanation.

B: It means that if you place a big order, we usually allow 3% for a trade discount.

A: It sounds good, and how about the quality? We only book for the best.

B: We always sell the best. Seeing is believing.

A: OK. How long does it take you to deliver if we order 500 cases of biscuits?

B: Within 2 weeks once we receive your orders. And concerning our financial position, credit standing and trade reputation, you may refer to Bank of Tianjin, or to our local Chamber of Commerce.

A: Thanks for your information. I have no doubt that establishing business relations will be to our mutual benefit.

B: So do I. I'm waiting for your specific inquiry.

Notes:

1. pamphlet 宣传册
2. line 行列,行业。比如：

I have been in the silk line for many years.

3. Your desire coincides with ours. 我们不谋而合。

4. competitive edge 竞争优势

5. meet with great favor 受欢迎

6. Seeing is believing. 眼见为实。

7. financial position, credit standing and trade reputation 财务状况、信用及声誉

8. Chamber of Commerce 商会

9. inquiry 询盘

Useful Patterns

1. You're welcome to visit our workshop at any time.
   欢迎您随时来工厂参观。

2. Having you got anything in mind you're interested in?
   有什么您感兴趣的产品吗?

3. By the courtesy of Mr. Black, we are given to understand the name and address of your firm.
   经由布莱克先生的引荐,我们才得知贵公司的大名和地址。

4. We are willing to enter into business relations with your firm.
   我方愿意与贵公司建立贸易关系。

5. We specialize in the export of Japanese Light Industrial Products and would like to trade with you in this line.
   我方专业出口日本轻工业产品,也诚挚希望与贵公司就此建立贸易关系。

6. Our mutual understanding and cooperation will certainly result in important business.
   双方相互理解与相互合作必将有助于我们进一步的贸易联系。

7. Your desire to establish business relations coincides with ours.

你方想要建立贸易关系的愿望与我方不谋而合。

8. —Is there anything I can help you with?
   —No, thanks. I am just browsing!
   ——有什么需要帮助的吗？
   ——不,谢谢,我只是随便看看!

9. We hope to do business with you on the basis of equality and mutual benefit.
   我方希望彼此的贸易联系是建立在平等和互利的基础上的。

10. I can send you a price list and a brochure of this series for your reference.
    现寄去该产品系列的价目表和宣传册供你方参考。

 Role – playing

1. Make a conversation between Mr. Smith, an importer from Britain, and Mr. Wang, a director of Qiqu Foodstuffs factory. Mr. Smith is visiting the sample room of the factory and Mr. Wang is accompanying him.

2. Your firm is dealing in silk products. A foreign company is interested in your silk scarf. They call you to inquire some detailed information. Now you are in charge of the reception of customers. Fulfill your task in three aspects:
   1) Warmly welcome and show your desire to enter into business relations;
   2) Explain the competitive advantages of the product, e.g. features, quality, and price;
   3) Invite further discussion on the deal.

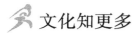 文化知更多

所有进出口贸易公司,如若对外寻求建立贸易关系,应以正式的商务信函告知对方,内容涵盖简要的公司及产品介绍、从何渠道获得信息

来源、表达建立贸易关系的愿望等。通常公司会随函附上产品目录和宣传册以供对方参考,并为今后潜在的询盘打下基础。信函范文如下:

Dear Sir or Madam:

  On the recommendation of your Chamber of Commerce, we have learned with pleasure the name and address of your company. We wish to inform you that we specialize in the export of Chinese silk products and shall be glad to enter into business relations with you on the basis of equality and mutual benefit.

  To give you a general idea of our products, we are sending you under separate cover a catalogue together with a range of pamphlets for your reference.

  Please let us have your specific enquiry if you are interested in any of the items listed in the catalogue. We shall make offers promptly.

  We look forward to your early reply.

Yours faithfully,
James Hu

Unit 3　Inquiry and Offer

Expected Goals

1. Understand some useful expressions on inquiry and offer, and try to make conversations of your own.
2. Practice business skills when dealing with inquiry and offer.

Lead-in

Generally, a business negotiation should go through four steps: inquiry, offer, counter-offer and acceptance. An inquiry is the buyer's request for information about certain commodity and the trade terms as well. It may be general or specific. A general inquiry usually involves the request for a catalogue, price list, sample, etc., while a specific inquiry includes such detailed information as specification of the goods, quality, quantity, price, discount, terms of payment, shipment, packing and insurance.

Offer and acceptance are the two essential aspects. An offer is the seller's promise to supply a certain commodity on terms and conditions. It may be firm or non-firm. Once a firm offer is accepted by the buyer, both the seller and the buyer have no right to revoke, alter or amend within its validity. A non-firm offer is usually subject to confirmation.

Situational Dialogues

Dialogne One Making an Inquiry

A—Mr. King   B—Mr. Lee

A: Mr. Lee, I'm pleased to have the opportunity of visiting your corporation. I hope to conclude some substantial business with you.

B: It's a great pleasure to meet you, Mr. King. You have just seen our exhibits in the showroom. May I know what particular items you're interested in?

A: I feel greatly interested in your baby biscuits. I've tried the samples and studied the catalogues. I think some of the items will find a ready market in the United States. Here is our inquiry list. Would you please quote us your most competitive price CIF Seattle?

B: Well, I'll look into your requirements first. You'd better tell us what quantity you require so that we can work out the offer?

A: I'll do that. Meanwhile, could you give me an indication of the price?

B: Here is our FOB price. All the prices in the list are subject to our confirmation.

A: What about commission, Mr. Lee? From European suppliers I usually get a 6%-10% commission for my imports. It's the general practice.

B: As a rule, we do not allow any commission. But if the order is a sizable one, we will consider it.

A: When can I have your firm CIF price, that is to say, the final offer, Mr. Lee?

B: Just wait, Mr. King. We'll have them worked out by tomorrow morning and inform you of the price as soon as possible. But please remember that our offer only remains open for 3 days.

A: Perfect. If your prices are agreeable and if I can get the commission I want, I can place the order right away.

Notes:

1. 国际贸易中使用的价格术语很多,其中以 FOB、CIF 及 CFR 三种价格术语最为常用。现将这三种价格术语扼要解释如下:

（1）FOB 价格叫装运港船上交货价,简称"船上交货"。FOB 是 Free On Board 的缩写。采用这一价格术语时要在其后注明装运港名称。

（2）CIF 价格叫成本加保险费、运费价。CIF 是 Cost Insurance Freight 的缩写。采用这种价格术语的时候,应在 CIF 后注明目的港名称。

（3）CFR 价格叫成本加运费价。采用这种价格术语时,也应在 CFR 后注明目的港名称。

2. make an inquiry 询盘

3. a ready market 市场畅销

4. quote 报价

5. work out the offer 报盘

6. subject to our confirmation 经由我方确认

7. commission 佣金

8. general practice 惯例

9. firm offer 实盘

10. place the order 下订单

Dialogue Two Make an Offer

A—Mr. King   B—Mr. Lee

A: Mr. Lee, I'm anxious to know about your offer.

B: Gladly. Thanks for your inquiry of August 3rd, Mr. King. We've been holding it for you. Here it is. Three hundred cases of baby biscuits, at 20 US dollars per kilogram, CIF Seattle. Shipment will be in November. You will notice the quotation is much lower than the current market price.

A: Is it firm?

B: Firm for 10 days.

A: Does it include any commission for us?

B: 5% commission for you. It is the most favorable price I can offer you, I guarantee, Mr. King. After all, it's the first time you order with me.

A: Yes, but it also means more repeat business for you. Is there any discount if I increase the quantity?

B: 3% discount for orders over 500 cases.

A: What kind of payment term do you usually accept?

B: We only accept L/C.

A: How long does it usually take you to make the delivery?

B: As a rule, we deliver all our orders within one month after receipt of the L/C. It takes longer, of course, for special orders. But in no case would it take longer than 3 months.

A: Fine. I hope my general manager will accept the above. I need to wait for his final confirmation.

A: When shall we hear from you?

B: Three days later.

B: I have to remind you that this offer expires on August 15th, after which there will be a sharp rise in price.

A: I see. I'll urge my boss to make a decision within the time limit.

Notes:

1. guarantee 保证
2. repeat business 回头客
3. L/C(全称为 letter of credit), 信用证
4. delivery 发货, 交付
5. expire 无效, 期满

Dialogue Three Counter-offer

A—Mr. King   B—Mr. Lee

A: Mr. Lee, my boss has gone over your price sheet, and still feels your prices are much too high. It will be difficult for us to make any sales.

B: I'm surprised to hear you say so, Mr. King. You know that the cost of production has been skyrocketing in recent years.

A: I'm afraid I can't agree with you there. Your quotation is really higher compared with others.

B: Ah, but everybody in the line of baby foods knows that ours is of prime quality, either in color or in flavor. In view of this, I should say the price is reasonable. So far the very fact that other clients keep on buying speaks for itself. If it weren't for our good relations, we wouldn't consider making you a firm offer at this price.

A: But I believe we'll have a hard time convincing our clients at your price. Well, to get the business done, let's consider making some concessions in our price.

B: Well, then, what's your idea of a competitive price?

A: On the basis of mutual benefit, I suggest somewhere around 15 US dollars per kilogram, CIF Seattle.

B: It's impossible for us to entertain your counter-offer, I'm afraid. The gap is too great.

A: How about meeting each other half way so that business can be concluded?

B: You certainly have a way of talking me into it, Mr. King. Your boss really got the right person. OK, if your order exceeds 300 cases, I'll reduce another 2 dollars. This is our rock-bottom price.

A: I'm glad we've come to an agreement on price. We'll go on to the other terms and conditions at our next meeting.

Notes:

1. counter-offer 还盘
2. skyrocket 猛然上涨
3. prime quality 优质货,上等货
4. make some concessions 让步
5. mutual benefit 互利
6. meet each other half way 折中,各让一步
7. talk into 说服
8. rock-bottom price 最低价

Useful Patterns

1. We would appreciate your sending us the latest samples with their best prices.
   请把贵公司的最新样品及最优惠的价格寄给我们,不胜感激。

2. I would like to have your lowest quotations, CIF Vancouver.
   希望您报成本加运费、保险费到温哥华的最低价格。

3. If your prices are favorable, I can place the order right away.
   如果你们的价格优惠,我们可以马上订货。

4. As there is a growing demand for this article, we have to ask you for a special discount.
   鉴于我方市场对此货的需求日增,务请你们考虑给予特别折扣。

5. As a rule, we deliver all our orders within 3 months after receipt of the covering letters of credit.
   一般来说,在收到相关信用证后三个月内我们就全部交货。

6. All the quotations on the list are subject to our final confirmation.
   报价单上的所有价格以我方最后确认为准。

7. I'm sorry. The difference between our price and your counter-offer is too wide.
   很遗憾,我们的价格与你方还盘之间的差距太大。

8. We can't accept your offer unless the price is reduced by 3%.
   除非你们减价3%,否则我们无法接受报盘。

9. This is our rock-bottom price, we can't make any further reduction.
   这是我方的最低价格,我们不能再让了。

10. As a rule, the larger the order, the lower the price.
    买得越多,价格越便宜,这是个惯例。

Role-playing

1. Suppose you are a representative of Longstar Imp. & Exp. Corporation. And you are very interested in the silk scarves of ABC Company at the Trade Fair. Please make an inquiry about their products' performance, price, delivery, etc.

2. Please make an offer for the goods based on the information below.
   Commodity: canned beef
   Quantity: 300 cases

Unit price: $ 200 per kilogram

Payment: by irrevocable L/C

Time of shipment: one month after receipt of the buyer's L/C

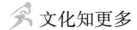
文化知更多

询盘范例:

Dear Sirs,

We are very much interested in importing baby dolls from Sydney.

We understand that you are a leading manufacturer and sales agent of baby toys in Canada. We shall appreciate it if you let us have detailed information about your products. Please send us your latest pamphlet and samples if possible.

We hope that this will be a good start for a long and profitable business relation between us.

Yours faithfully,
× × ×

还盘范例:

Dear James,

We are glad to learn from your letter of July 3rd that you are interested in our baby dolls. Enclosed please find the catalogue and price list you asked for, and details of our terms of payment and time of shipment.

On purchases exceeding a total of :

—US $ 10,000 but not exceeding US $ 30,000—8%

—US $ 30,000 but not exceeding US $ 60,000—15%

—US $ 60,000 and above—20%

No special allowance could be given on a total purchase below US $ 10,000.

Yours faithfully,
× × ×

Unit 4 Packing and Insurance

 Expected Goals

1. Understand some useful expressions on packing and insurance, and try to make conversations of your own.
2. Be familiar with common packing manners and insurance types when dealing with international logistics.

 Lead-in

It has been estimated that as much as 70% of all cargo loss could be prevented by proper packaging and marking. Hence, suitable packing is of great necessity and significance. Indeed, packing aims to provide exact information about the goods inside, and make the products appealing. More important, the real art of packing is to get the contents into nice, compact shape that will stay in perfect condition with nothing missing during the roughest journey. When choosing the ways of packing, sellers should take into account such factors as the features of goods, the mode of transportation, the regulations of the import and export countries, the requirement of the buyer and the like.

Marine insurance is defined as a contract of insurance whereby the insurance in return for premiums collected undertakes to indemnify the insured in a manner and to the extent thereby agreed, against marine losses. The parties involved in marine insurance are insurer, the insured, and an insurance broker. According to People's Insurance Company of China Ocean Marine Cargo Clauses, the main marine insurance is classified as Basic Insurance Coverage and Additional Insurance Coverage. All Risks, FPA., and WPA that we are familiar with are the common ways used in international trade.

Situational Dialogues

Dialogue One   Packing (1)

A—Mr. King   B—Mr. Lee

A: As for last week's order, I must say I'm very satisfied with it. You're so considerate, Mr. Lee. But the packing is also of great importance.

B: Definitely, Mr. King. Now we'll talk about the packing.

A: As is known to all, foodstuff has its own specialty. We have to take many details into consideration.

B: You may rest assured of that. We'll pack the goods in compliance with your request.

A: Firstly, the packing must be strong enough to bear rough handling.

B: Yes, I'm sure this cardboard can stand a lot of jolting in transit.

A: Cardboard? Oh, I'm afraid it's not strong enough. I don't want to take any chances.

B: We'll provide seaworthy packing and we also don't want to cause a lot of inconvenience to our customers.

A: That sounds great. But what does seaworthy packing mean?

B: Oh, each carton lined with plastic sheets is waterproof and as the boxes are made of cardboard, they will be handled with care.

A: That would be better. We also have inner package of each small unit so that it can't be spoiled by dampness or rain.

B: Strong packing will ensure the goods against any possible damage during transit.

A: Glad to hear that. Your outer packing is really superior to your competitors'. But I'm still worried about the inner packing. The eye-catching appearance of the biscuit must help push the sales.

B: Indeed. Please look at this design. Don't you think it's so lovely that all the children can't move their eyes away when they see it?

A: Oh, so lovely! I think my boy will be one of them.

B: Thanks for your approval.

A: Undoubtedly your service always meets the customer's demand. But the final decision has to be made by our general manager.

B: That's OK. I'll be waiting for your reply.

Notes:

1. considerate 考虑周到的
2. in compliance with your request 符合你方要求
3. bear rough handling 承受粗糙搬运
4. cardboard 纸板箱
5. jolting 震动,颠簸
6. I don't want to take any chances. 我可不想冒险。

7. seaworthy packing 适合海运的包装

8. Each carton lined with plastic sheets is waterproof. 纸箱内都附有塑料布,可以防水。

9. be handled with care 小心搬运

10. be spoiled by dampness or rain 因为潮湿或雨水而受损

11. eye-catching appearance 吸引眼球的外表

Dialogue Two　Packing（2）

A—Mr. King　　B—Mr. Lee

A: Mr. Lee, I have connected our general manager and he has known the detailed information about our packing. He basically agrees on it, but still has some suggestions.

B: Many thanks to your manager, Mr. King, and I'd like to cock my ears to listen.

A: OK. He suggested that the cardboard should be strengthened with double straps.

B: Obviously, packing in sturdy cases is essential and all these cases will be secured with strapping.

A: He's also worried about that the possible jolting, squeezing during transportation. Customers usually prefer the perfect package. They can't bear any flaws appeared on their new goods.

B: We have already taken it into account. So it's necessary to add pallet package. As you know, Mr. King, pallet is suitable for loading and unloading, moving and storing by machines.

A: Then it will be no danger of anything going wrong. Thanks for your understanding.

B: Anything else?

A: Yes, Mr. Lee. You know our goods will be transshipped in Singapore. We hope there are details of weights, symbols of warnings and directions, as well as shipping marks on each case.

B: No problem. Actually because of our goods' special characteristics, we add both shock proof and damp proof directions on the surface of each case in order to avoid any possible damages.

A: How thoughtful you are!

B: OK, I've written down your suggestions and I'm sure we'll meet your needs. But the charge of packing should be borne by buyers. This is international practice.

A: I agree with it beyond question. It's for our account. Let's talk about it now.

Notes:

1. cock my ears to listen 洗耳恭听

2. The cardboard should be strengthened with double strap. 纸板箱外应该用双道箱带捆扎。

3. sturdy 坚固的

4. squeezing 挤压

5. pallet package 托盘包装

6. shipping marks 装箱唛头

7. shock proof and damp proof directions 抗震和防潮标识

8. international practice 国际惯例

9. for one's account 由某方承担

Dialogue Three Insurance

A—Mr. King   B—Mr. Lee

A: Mr. Lee, I'm very glad that we have settled the problem about packing and may I have the opportunity to discuss something concerning insurance?

B: With respect to insurance, we generally insure with the People's Insurance Company of China (PICC). At present they have about 300 cargo surveying and claim settling agents in more than 90 countries and regions.

A: Does PICC have an agent in our region?

B: Yes, of course. The agent there has the authority to effect settlement locally.

A: It will be very convenient for us to lodge a claim if there is any damage taking place during transportation. Frankly speaking, I hope everything goes smoothly.

B: It obviously will. But we should prepare well in advance to nip in the bud.

A: Yes. Would you please introduce your insurance coverages to me?

B: The three basic coverages we often employ are Free from Particular Average (FPA), With Particular Average (WPA) and All Risks.

A: As for our order, which one would you choose to effect?

B: WPA would be our preference.

A: After our discussion about packing, I feel so confident that our goods will be delivered without any serious damage. But it doesn't mean that it's unnecessary to insure against Fresh and Rainwater Damage as well as TPND.

B: In that case, it would be better to cover All Risks. And the clause will be written in our contract: Insurance is to be covered by the sellers for 110% of invoice value against All Risks as per Ocean Marine Cargo Clause of the People's Insurance Company of China dated Jan. 1st, 2014.

A: OK. How about the premium?

B: Although our deal is conducted on the basis of CIF, the extra premium should be borne by the buyer.

A：It's worth bearing the cost.
B：That's settled.

Notes：

1. insure *vt.* 投保,保险;insurance *n.* 常见搭配有：

cover insurance/effect insurance/arrange insurance/provide insurance/take out insurance

insurance 后介词的用法：

（1）表示投保的险别。后接 against。如：insurance against All Risks

（2）表示保额。后接 for。如：insurance for 110% of the invoice value

（3）表示保险率或费率,后接 at。如：insurance at the rate of 5%

（4）表示向某保险公司投保,后接 with。如：insurance with PICC

2. with respect to 关于

3. cargo surveying and claim settling agents 货物检验和理赔代理

4. lodge a claim 提出索赔

5. nip in the bud 防患于未然

6. coverage 险别

7. Free from Particular Average, With Particular Average and All Risks 平安险、水渍险和全险

8. TPND(Theft,Pilferage and Non-Delivery) 偷窃、提货不着险

9. invoice value 发票金额

10. premium 保险费

Useful Patterns

1. The outer packing should be suitable for long-distance ocean transportation.
   外包装应该是适合长途海运的。

2. They would ask for compensation on the grounds of faulty packing.
   他们会以包装有瑕疵而要求赔偿。

on the ground(s) of 以……为理由

3. The outer packing in bales or in wooden cases is at buyer's option.
   外包装打包还是使用木箱,由买方选择。

4. As to the inner packaging, it must be attractive and helpful to the sales.
   至于内包装,必须具有吸引力,且有利于促销。

5. Please make sure that the packing is strong enough to stand rough handling.
   请确保包装牢固,能够承受粗鲁装卸。

6. The machines must be well protected against dampness, moisture, rust and shock.
   机器包装必须防湿、防潮、防锈、防震。

7. We have covered insurance on 800 cases of canned beef for 110% of the invoice value against All Risks.
   我们已将八百箱罐装牛肉按发票金额的百分之一百一十投保一切险。

8. The more the required cover, the higher the premium rate.
   保险类别越多,保险费率就越高。

9. And the extra premium involved will be for the buyer's account.
   由此产生的额外保险费应由买方负责。

10. But as a rule, we do not cover them unless the buyers want to.
    不过按照惯例,除非买方要求,否则我们不投保这些险别。

Role-playing

1. Suppose you and the seller are holding a negotiation about the packing of newly-ordered books. Please discuss their packing manners, shipping marks and indicative marks.

2. Make up a dialogue about the insurance of these newly-ordered

books, including insurance company, coverage, premium, etc.

文化知更多

国际海运中货物保险主要险别有:

（一）基本险

基本险包括3种险别,按责任大小排序依次为:

（1）平安险（Free from Particular Average,FPA）

自然灾害如恶劣气候、海啸、地震、洪水等;或下列原因造成的全部或部分损失:搁浅、触礁、沉没、互撞、失火、爆炸等;装卸或转运时由于货物落海的施救费用;避难港、中途港由卸货、存仓以及运送货物产生的特别费用;共同海损的牺牲、分推和救助费用等。

（2）水渍险（With Particular Average,WPA）

平安险＋平安险所列自然灾害所造成的部分损失。

（3）一切险（All Risk）

水渍险＋一般附加险。

（二）附加险

附加险又可分为一般附加险和特别附加险:

（1）一般附加险（General Additional Risk）

一般附加险包括:① 偷窃、提货不着险;② 淡水雨淋险;③ 短量险;④ 混杂、沾污险;⑤ 渗漏险;⑥ 碰损、破碎险;⑦ 串味险;⑧ 受潮受热险;⑨ 钩损险;⑩ 包装破裂险;⑪ 锈损险。

（2）特别附加险（Specific Additional Risk）

如:海运货物战争险、罢工险等。

Unit 5 Shipment and Payment

Expected Goals

1. Understand important expressions and typical sentences on shipment and payment, and try to make conversations of your own.
2. Students are required to know terms of shipment, how to effect payment in international trade, and the advantages of E-bank payment.

Background Information

Delivering goods to the buyer is one of the seller's major obligations under the sales contract. Originally, the term "shipment" is "the loading of goods on a ship." However, in actual trading practice today, shipment can also be made by air, rail, truck and parcel post. The choice of shipping methods depends on the nature of the products, the distance to be shipped, available means of transportation, and relative freight costs. Terms of shipment usually cover time of shipment, port of shipment and port of destination, transshipment and partial shipments, conditions of shipment, etc.

Terms of payment define the conditions under which the seller and the buyer agree to settle the financial amount of the sales contract. It is directly related to the benefits of both sides of the buyer and the seller. The method of payment for each transaction is to be agreed upon between the two trading parties at the time of placing an order. Generally, there are three commonly used methods: L/C (letter of credit), collection and remittance. With the development of Internet and modern E-commerce, Online Payment is used widely.

 Situational Dialogues

Dialogne One　Shipment (1)

A—Mr. King　　B—Mr. Lee

A: It seems that our talks proceed very smoothly. Shipment is our another concern.

B: Yes, Mr. King, it's of great importance to choose the suitable means of transportation. So which one do you prefer, by sea or by air?

A: I know shipping the goods by air is the quickest and safest way. But the cost might be quite a bit more and the retail price must be influenced by it.

B: Every coin has two sides. So you mean...

A: Mr. Lee, we decide to ship goods by sea. Would you please show me the shipping costs of several shipping companies which you have business connections?

B: MAERSK's offer is $ 1,680 per 20-foot container, COSCO's (China

Ocean Shipping Company's) is ＄1,600, APL's (American President Lines) is ＄1,580.

A: Oh, the costs of them are all over my budget, Mr. Lee. The prices are 20% higher than those of some small shipping companies.

B: Small shipping companies? They often receive customers' complaints about their poor services. Don't you want to risk being delayed by employing them?

A: We also heard of some annoying complaints.

B: But such shipping companies as MAERSK enjoy good reputations worldwide. They can guarantee the prompt transshipment.

A: You surely know that transshipment adds to the expenses and sometimes may delay the arrival. So it's very essential to choose a reliable shipping company, otherwise we have no competitive superiority.

B: I understand you. That's why I offer you some famous shipping companies.

A: Is the shipping space easy to be booked?

B: It depends on your final decision. The earlier of your order, the easier of our booking.

A: OK, in order to secure the safety and punctual delivery of our goods and to avoid some unnecessary troubles, I'd like to select MAERSK.

B: Agreed. We'll try our best to effect shipment as soon as possible.

Notes:

1. proceed smoothly 进展顺利
2. Every coin has two sides. 硬币有正反两面,意指事情有利必有弊。
3. MAERSK/ COSCO/ APL(船公司名称)马士基/中远/美国总统号
4. budget 预算
5. guarantee 保证
6. transshipment 转船

7. superiority 优越性

8. punctual delivery 即期交货

Dialogue Two　Shipment（2）

A—Mr. King　　B—Mr. Lee

A：Mr. Lee, compared with other exporter's service, yours is really of high quality.

B：Thanks. Our good reputation also needs our customers' cooperation. With respect to the delivery time, I'd like to have your requirement.

A：You know the Christmas season is approaching. The prompt delivery can catch the peak season for this commodity in our market. So is it possible to deliver them in October?

B：But I'm afraid I can't promise you any October delivery. You may look at our orders. Most of them have the same demand as yours. It's really a hard nut to crack.

A：I understand. When is the earliest possible date you can ship the goods?

B：The earliest shipment we can effect is early November.

A：I'm afraid it's too late. Christmas season starts from November. It will take us at least two weeks before the goods can reach our retailers.

B：We'll feel sorry to bring trouble to our customers. If partial shipment is allowed, we'll try our best to advance our shipment to early October.

A：It sounds reasonable. How much can we expect in the first shipment?

B：One third of the order that you're going to place will be shipped in about early October.

A: OK. This portion can meet the urgent need of our clients, but temporarily.

B: Once we effect the first shipment, we'll lose no time getting the goods ready for the second lot.

A: What about the third lot? I mean the last one.

B: The third lot should be made at the beginning of November. And MAERSK can assure the punctual delivery time. That's why I recommend it to you.

A: So it's worth choosing a big shipping company. You know if the goods can not reach the market in time, then good quality and competitive price would be meaningless.

B: Hope everything is smooth. And expanding our business in your area depends on our cooperation.

A: That'll be OK. Please let us know if you effect the first shipment.

B: Yes, Mr. King, we'll keep you informed.

Notes:

1. with respect to 关于
2. peak season for this commodity 商品销售的旺季
3. a hard nut to crack 很难解决的问题
4. partial shipment 分批装运
5. temporarily 暂时
6. lose no time doing sth. 及早,尽快做某事
7. recommend 推荐

Dialogue Three　Payment

A—Mr. King　　B—Mr. Lee

A: Mr. Lee, packing, insurance and shipment are all satisfactory. Let's go into the payment terms. Which one does your company accept?

B: Well, we only accept payment in irrevocable letter of credit payable against shipping documents.

A: Opening the L/C is very costly and ties up our funds.

B: We are so confident about our product's quality and popularity. The quick turnover will compensate your cost on L/C.

A: Maybe. But how about make further concessions in order to conclude the transaction?

B: I do hope so, Mr. King. But there's no exception these years, since the international market is not stable as before.

A: We have enjoyed good reputation in the field of importing. Would you please allow payment by D/P in view of our long-term business relationship?

B: Just because we cherish our good relationship, I can make some compromise. But I'll be in a pickle in that case.

A: How about 50% by D/P and 50% by L/C?

B: I have no right to allow you 50% by D/P. The only thing that I can do is 30% by D/P. Let's meet each other halfway, OK?

A: If I say no…

B: Then I have to say I regret that we can't conduct the deal.

A: All right. I venture to say you are really good at persuading.

B: Thank you. Your support and understanding help me a lot. I want to create a win-win situation.

A: I agree with you.

Notes：

1. irrevocable letter of credit 不可撤销信用证

   establish / open / issue a Letter of Credit 开立信用证

2. ties up our funds 套牢资金

3. turnover 营业额,成交量

4. conclude the transaction 达成交易

5. make some concessions/compromise 做出让步,妥协

6. D/P(Documents against payment) 付款交单

   D/A (Documents against Acceptance) 承兑交单

7. in a pickle 身陷困境,惹麻烦

8. venture to do sth. 冒昧地做某事

9. a win-win situation 双赢的局面

Useful Patterns

1. How do you like the goods dispatched, by railway or by sea?
   贵方想要怎样发货,铁路运输还是海洋运输?

2. As a rule, we deliver all our orders within three months after receipt of the covering L/C.
   一般说来,我们在收到有关的信用证后三个月内可交货。

3. The prompt delivery can catch the peak season for this commodity in our market.
   即期交货可以赶上市场中商品的销售旺季。

4. We shall make shipment within the time the contract stipulates.
   我方将在合同规定的期限内装船。

5. May I suggest we effect shipment in three equal lots, starting from May?
   可否建议我们从五月份开始分相等的三批办理装运?

6. Our terms of payment are by a confirmed irrevocable letter of credit by draft at sight.
   我们的支付方式是以保兑不可撤销的、凭即期汇票支付的信用证。

7. To open an L/C will add to the cost of our import.
   开立信用证会增加我方进口货物的成本。

8. I'd like to discuss the terms of payment with you. I wonder if you would accept D/P.

我想同你讨论一下付款条件。不知你能否接受付款交单的方式。

9. For the sake of friendship, we can only accept 30% cash payment in US dollars.

鉴于双方友谊,我方同意你方以美金支付30%的货款。

Role-playing

1. Suppose you and the seller are holding a negotiation about the packing of the shipment of canned beef. Please discuss the details of the goods such as shipping manners (partial shipment or transshipment), shipping time, cost, etc.
2. Make up a dialogue about the payment of canned beef, and explain to the seller why you insist on payment by L/C instead of D/P.

文化知更多

外贸常用的付款方式有三种:

(1) 信用证(Letter of Credit, L/C)

(2) 汇付,主要包括电汇(Telegraphic Transfer, T/T)、信汇(Mail Transfer, M/T)和票汇(Demand Draft, D/D)三种

(3) 托收(Collection),主要包括付款交单(Documents against Payment, D/P)和承兑交单(Documents against Acceptance, D/A)两种

D/P是我们发货后准备好议付单据,通过我方银行交单至客户方银行,客户银行提示客户单据已到,客户付款后银行交单。D/A则是通过我方银行交单给客户银行,不同的是客人只需承兑我方单据,就可以拿走正本单据,到期后再付款。

D/P、D/A的付款方式采用得较少。主要由于出口公司能否收到货

款,完全取决于进口商的信用。进口商能否保时、保质、保量收到货物也取决于出口商的信用。对于信用好的进口商,一般不会出现不付货款的现象,遇到信用差的进口商,常常发生拖欠或拒付货款现象。因此,D/P 和 D/A 多用于信誉比较好的进出口商。

Unit 6   Seeing off Business Clients

Expected Goals

1. Understand the process of sightseeing, farewell dinner, check-out and seeing off at the airport when dealing with foreign guests.
2. Skillfully apply useful expressions concerning seeing off business clients to daily conversations.

Lead-in

Bidding farewell marks the end of entertaining foreign guests. Wherever it is arranged to be, at the dinner table, or at any other places such as the airport, seaport, railway station, etc, it is as equally important as the welcome activities and therefore should be conducted sincerely. If anything undesirable happens at the last minute, it may ruin the entire experience of a tour.

Generally speaking, farewell activities consist of sightseeings, shopping for valuable souvenirs, holding farewell dinners, checking out of the hotel and seeing off business clients at the airport. During their stay, a qualified local receptionist should be thoughtful and enthusiastic. He or she is responsible for making the farewell experience impressive and everlasting throughout his or her service. Of course, specific arrangement, to a great extent, depends on the special features of a specific group, but the whole process is usually flooded with beautiful memories and wishes.

 Situational Dialogues

Dialogue One　　Concluding a Business

A—Mr. Lee　　B—Mr. King

A: I'm so happy that we've reached an agreement on all the terms after a long-time negotiation. Mr. King, if you are not against, we'll draft two originals of the sales contract right away, and sign it then.

B: By all means. Both of our parties do have made great efforts. I believe it will bear fruit in no time. How about holding a signing ceremony, Mr. Lee? Our general manager from the United States will be present.

A: That would be my pleasure.

B: And we can publicize our organic baby food by inviting some journalists.

A: Good idea. I'll inform you of the detailed arrangement soon. Oh, Mr. King, it is the first time you have come to Tianjin, isn't it?

B: Exactly. Tianjin is really a nice place, full of traditional and modern flavor.

A: Well, if you don't mind, I'm honored to be your tour guide for sight-

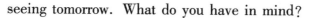

seeing tomorrow. What do you have in mind?

B: Aha, I've been waiting for it so long, and I'm keen on Tianjin's distinctive customs and specialties. Equally important, I'd like to find some meaningful souvenirs for my friends in the U.S.

A: OK. I'll do my utmost to satisfy all your wishes. Have a sound sleep, Mr. King. Tomorrow will be a busy day.

B: I very much appreciate your kindness. See you tomorrow.

Notes:

1. reach an agreement 达成共识
2. term 条款(此外还可表示学期、任期、术语等含义)
3. originals of the sales contract 销售合同正本
4. by all means 完全同意
5. publicize 宣传
6. sightseeing 观光
7. specialty 特产
8. souvenir 纪念品
9. appreciate 感激(此外还可表示欣赏、珍惜等含义)

Dialogue Two　　Arranging Sightseeing

A—Mr. Lee　　B—Mr. King

A: Good morning, Mr. King. Sightseeing is our agenda today.

B: Fantastic! Where shall we go first?

A: Based on your needs, I'll take you on a quick tour of the downtown area of Tianjin. There you may feel its modern rhythm.

B: Yes. I always pay close attention to the development of China's costal cities. Since the successful holding of Davo's Economic Forum in Binhai New Area, Tianjin has taken on a new look. It has become a modern urban scenic spot, complete with tours, leisure and entertainment.

A: You know better than me, Mr. King. I therefore encourage you to visit here more often. This way, you will get to know a colorful Tianjin, constantly developing and changing. And after the lunch in Food Street, we can pay a visit to Ancient Culture Street for souvenirs. It will be a treasure-hunting journey, which opens a window for Tianjin's ancient civilization, I promise.

B: Exactly my thought. What can we get then?

A: The shops along the street sell all kinds of antiques which reflect Chinese tradition and culture. As well, a variety of local delicate handcrafts were on display, such as clay figurines, kites, papercuts, embroidery and the like.

B: That's what I really want. Can we bargain there?

A: Er...Sometimes we can, but sometimes the price is fixed. Later in the evening, we may enjoy a fine scenery of Haihe River by boat. Believe me, and definitely it won't let you down.

B: OK, I can't wait. Many thanks for your hospitality.

Notes:

1. downtown 市中心,商业区
2. rhythm 节奏,韵律
3. Davo's Economic Forum 达沃斯经济论坛
4. take on a new look 焕然一新
5. Food Street 天津南市食品街
6. Ancient Culture Street 天津古文化街
7. treasure-hunting 寻宝
8. civilization 文明
9. handcraft 手工制品
10. on display 在展出

11. clay figurines 泥人彩塑
12. embroidery 刺绣
13. bargain 讨价还价
14. let sb. down 使某人失望
15. hospitality 热情好客

Dialogue Three Check-out

A—Mr. King   B—Receptionist of Tianjin Hotel

A: Excuse me, I'd like to check out today.

B: Your room number please, sir?

A: Oh, my room number is 203 and here is the key.

B: OK, just wait a moment. Sorry to have kept you waiting. Here is your bill, 2,300 RMB yuan altogether. Please sign on the print.

A: Could I pay by credit card?

B: Certainly. And Mr. King, please feel free to add your opinions and suggestions to this card so that our hotel can further improve our service.

A: Oh, I really enjoyed my stay here with cozy rooms and considerate services.

B: Thanks for your appreciation. You are always welcome to our hotel.

Notes:

1. check out 办理酒店退房手续, 或下飞机离开机场
   (反之, check in 可表示办理酒店入住手续, 或办理机场登机手续)
2. bill 账单
3. credit card 信用卡
4. feel free to 随意, 随时
5. cozy room 舒适的房间

Dialogue Four　　Seeing off Business Clients

A—Mr. King　　B—Mr. Lee

A: How time flies! Mr. Lee, I have to say goodbye to you and all the friends present. It's very kind of you to see me off at the airport.

B: It's my pleasure. Mr. King, is there anything I can do for you before your departure? Please let me know if I can be of any help.

A: Nothing else. It has been a very pleasant and productive trip for me. Your company impressed me most, and I was moved by your support and hospitality. I believe our cooperation will be successful.

B: That's for sure. I'm glad you enjoyed your stay here. By the way, I'm obliged to remind you of checking in at Business Class over there. Your flight will be boarding at Gate 5 at 10 o'clock. Please pass through security no later than 9:20.

A: OK, I'll bear in mind.

B: Keep your ticket and passport, and not to leave your luggage unattended. Mr. King, this is your departure card. Please fill it out and hand it in at the immigration desk.

A: Lee, you are so thoughtful. We'll keep in touch.

B: Sure. Hope to see you again, and have a nice trip.

…

Broadcast: Good morning! Ladies and gentlemen, may I please note that Flight number BA236 is now boarding. Please bring your belongings by Gate 5 on the plane. I wish you a pleasant journey, thank you.

Notes:

1. see sb. off 送别某人
2. departure 离开

3. That's for sure. 那是当然。

4. be obliged to do sth. 不得不，必须

5. business class 商务舱，头等舱

   （类似的表达还有：economy class 经济舱）

6. board the plane 登机

7. pass through security 接受安检

8. Don't leave your luggage unattended. 请看管好你的行李。

9. departure card 出境卡

10. immigration desk 移民登记处

11. belongings 个人财物

Useful Patterns

1. Excuse me, I will leave today. I'd like to pay my bill now.
   您好，打扰一下，今天我想退房。请给我结账。

2. —How would you like to make the payment, Miss Zhang?
   —Credit cards. May I use my visa card?
   ——张女士，您想用什么方式付款？
   ——信用卡。我可以用 Visa 卡吗？

3. It's very kind of you to come to see me off.
   谢谢你来送我。

4. Thank you for taking time off from your busy jobs to come here tonight to say goodbye to Mr. King.
   感谢你们今晚从百忙之中抽空到这儿向金先生道别。

5. Is there anything else I can do for you before your departure?
   你离开前还有什么需要我帮忙的吗？

6. I very much appreciate everything you have done for me. I really don't know how to thank you.
   非常感谢你为我所做的一切。真的不知道该怎么样感谢你。

7. Don't mention it. I'm sure your visit will help to promote the friendship and understanding between both of us.

   别放在心上。我相信您的来访一定会加强我们之间的友谊和相互理解。

8. The queue is long. This one could go on as carry-on luggage if you like.

   排队的人太多了。如果你愿意,这件可以当作手提行李带上飞机。

9. If you're ever in Sydney again, you must look me up.

   如果您下次有机会再来悉尼,请一定要联系我们。

10. I hope you will have a nice trip home. And please give my best wishes to your family.

    今天天气不错,祝你们回家旅途愉快。替我给你的家人带去我最美好的祝福。

Role-playing

1. Suppose your business partner will leave for another place to work. Now please see her off at the railway station and send her a silk scarf to express your gratitude and friendship.

2. You are holding a farewell dinner for your business client from the U.S. Make up a dialogue including your negotiation fruit, your gratitude and everlasting friendship.

文化知更多

访问日程一般应由接待方首先提出。日程草案拟订后,可先将主要内容告知对方,以便听取对方意见,并使对方有所准备。日程安排的松紧应适当。活动安排太少,让客人有时在宾馆里无所事事,会感到受冷遇;活动安排太多,又会令客人筋疲力尽。要尽量使客人在工作以外的时间内,多看一些东西,多接触一些人,既感到充实,也能得到适度的休息。日程安排的好坏,对访问的成功与顺利进行具有重要的意义。因此,在拟订日程草案时,除了遵循通常的礼仪程序以外,还要考虑以下一些因素:

(1) 访问的目的和性质

(2) 来访者的愿望

(3) 来访者过去是否曾经来访过,哪些项目过去已经看过,如何使本次访问更具特色

(4) 来访者的年龄及身体状况能适应的活动限度

(5) 来访者的文化背景和宗教信仰等

物流用基础词汇

freight rates	运费率
freight absorption	运费免收
volume of freight	货运量
freight agent	运输行
freight car	[美](一节)货车
freight engine	货运机车
freight house	货栈,堆栈
freight ton [tonnage]	容积吨(数)
freight-in n. (=freight inward, transportation-in)	进货运费
freight-out n. (=freight outward, transportation-out)	销货运费
freight forward	运费由提货人支付
freight paid	运费付讫
freight prepaid (=advanced freight)	运费先付
dead freight	空舱费;空舱;不易腐坏

	的大件货物
additional freight	增列运费，附加运费
advanced freight	预付运费
air freight	航空运费
back goods freight	退货费用
bulk freight	散装货物
collect freight	待收运费，收取运费
cost and freight	离岸加运费价格
direct freight	直航运费
distance freight	增加距离运费
fast freight	快运货物
general freight	普通货物
home freight	返回运费，回程运费
inbound freight	到达货物
inflammable freight	易燃货物
interline freight	铁路联运货物
less-than-carload freight（LCL freight）	零担货物
lump sum freight	按整船计算的运费，包干运费
manifest freight	快运货物
measurement freight	按体积计算的运费
multiple freight	复式运费
net freight	运费纯收入，运费实收金，运费净数
open freight	自由运费，未定运费
outbound freight	运出货物
outward freight	销出运费
overland freight	陆运货运

package freight	包裹货运，零担货物
quick dispatch freight	快运货物
refused freight	收货人拒收的货物
restricted freight	限制条件下运输的货物（如易燃品、易爆品等）
return cargo freight	回运货物运费
shipping freight	运费
shortfall freight	亏舱运费
through freight	直达运费，联运货物
freight to be collected	运到收费，运费待收
freight to be deducted	应扣代付运费

商务篇常见缩略语

AFB（AIR FREIGHT BILL）	空运提单
C&F（cost & freight）	成本加运费价
D/P（document against payment）	付款交单
D/A（document against acceptance）	承兑交单
CO（certificate of origin）	一般原产地证
GSP（generalized system of preferences）	普惠制
CTN/CTNS（carton/cartons）	纸箱
PCE/PCS（piece/pieces）	只、个、支等
DL/DLS（dollar/dollars）	美元
DOZ/DZ（dozen）	一打
PKG（package）	一包,一捆,一扎,一件等
WT（weight）	重量
GW（gross weight）	毛重
NW（net weight）	净重
（customs declaration）	报关单

EA（each）	每个,各
W（with）	具有
w/o（without）	没有
FAC（facsimile）	传真
IMP（import）	进口
EXP（export）	出口
MAX（maximum）	最大的、最大限度的
MIN（minimum）	最小的,最低限度
M/V（merchant vessel）	商船
S.S（steamship）	船运
MT 或 M/T（metric ton）	公吨
DOC（document）	文件、单据
INT（international）	国际的
P/L（packing list）	装箱单、明细表
INV（invoice）	发票
PCT（percent）	百分比
REF（reference）	参考、查价
EMS（express mail special）	特快专递
STL（style）	式样、款式、类型
T 或 LTX 或 TX（telex）	电传
T/T（TELEGRAPHIC TRANSFER）	电汇
R.S.V.P.（REPONDEZ S'IL VOUS PLAIT）	静候函复
RMB（renminbi）	人民币
S/M（shipping marks）	装船标记
PR 或 PRC（price）	价格
PUR（purchase）	购买、购货
S/C（sales contract）	销售确认书
L/C（letter of credit）	信用证

B/L（bill of lading）	提单
FOB（free on board）	离岸价
CIF（cost, insurance & freight）	成本、保险加运费价
CARR. PD.（CARRIAGE PAID）	运费已付
C. B. D.（CASH BEFORE DELIVERY）	付现后交货
CONSGT（CONSIGNMENT）	委托销售
SGD（SIGNED）	已签署
SHPD（SHIPPED）	已装船
S. T.（SHORT TON）	短吨

Appendix

Ⅰ. Insurance Policy（保险单）

中国人民财产保险股份有限公司货物运输保险单
PICC PROPERTY AND CASUALTY COMPANY
LIMITED CARGO TRANSPORTATION INSURANCE POLICY

总公司设于北京　　　　一九四九年创立
Head Office：Beijing　　Established in 1949

印刷号（Printed Number）
保险单号（Policy No. ）
合同号（Contract NO. ）
发票号（Invoice NO. ）
信用证号（L／C NO. ）
被保险人（Insured）

中国人民财产保险股份有限公司(以下简称本公司)根据被保险人的要求,以被保险人向本公司缴付约定的保险费为对价,按照本保险单列明条款承保下述货物运输保险,特订立本保险单。
THIS POLICY OF INSURANCE WITNESSES THAT PICC PROPERTY AND CASUALTY COMPANY LIMITED (HEREINAFTER CALLED "THE COMPANY") AT THE REQUEST OF THE INSURED AND IN CONSIDERATION OF THE AGREED PREMIUM PAID TO THE COMPANY BY THE INSURED, UNDERTAKES TO INSURE THE UNDERMENTIONED GOODS IN TRANSPORTATION SUBJECT TO THE CONDITION OF THIS POLICY AS PER THE CLAUSES PRINTED BELOW.

标记与号码 MARKS & NOS.	包装及数量 PACKING AND QUANTITY	保险货物项目 GOODS	保险金额 AMOUNT INSURED

总保险金额(Total Amount Insured) _____
保费(Premium)：_____
启运日期(Date of Commencement)：_____
装载运输工具(Per Conveyance)：_____
自：_____ 经：_____ 到：_____
From：_____ Via：_____ To：_____
承保险别(Conditions)：

所保货物，如发生保险单项下可能引起索赔的损失，应立即通知本公司或下述代理人查勘。如有索赔，应向本公司提交正本保险单(本保险单共有_____份正本)及有关文件，如一份正本已用于索赔，其余正本自动失效。

IN THE EVENT OF LOSS OR DAMAGE WHICH MAY RESULT IN A CLAIM UNDER THIS POLICY, IMMEDIATE NOTICE MUST BE GIVEN TO THE COMPANY OR AGENT AS MENTIONED. CLAIMS, IF ANY, ONE OF THE ORIGINAL POLICY WHICH HAS BEEN ISSUED IN _____ ORIGINAL(S) TOGETHER WITH THE RELEVENT DOCUMENTS ALL BE SURRENDERED TO THE COMPANY. IF ONE OF THE ORIGINAL POLICY HAS BEEN ACCOMPLISHED, THE OTHERS TO BE VOID.

保险人(Underwriter)：_____
电话(Tel)：_____

传真(FAX)：_____

地址(ADD)：_____

赔款偿付地点(Claim Payable at)：_____

签单日期(Issuing Date)：_____

授权人签字(Authorized Signature)：_____

核保人：_____ 制单人：_____ 经办人：_____

Ⅱ Packing List(装箱单)

装箱单 PACKING LIST

唛头
SHIPPING MARK：

日期
DATE：

订舱号
SO No.：

发票号
INVOICE NO.：

收货人
CONSIGNEE：

合同号
CONTRACT NO.：

由 FROM：

至 TO：

品名	箱数	数量	单位	重量 Weight			
				毛重 Gross		净重 Net	
DESCRIPTION	CTN NO.	QTY.	UNIT	每箱	总毛重	每箱	总净重
				PER CTN	TOTAL	PER CTN	TOTAL
				单位 UNIT：(公斤 KG)			
Total							

Ⅲ. Commercial Invoice(商业发票)

COMMERCIAL INVOICE

Issuer

Invoice No. : _____

Invoice Date: _____

To

S/C No. : _____

L/C No. : _____

Terms of
Payment: _____

Transport Details:
From _____ To _____ Via _____
By _____

Marks and Numbers	Number and kind of package Description of goods	Quantity	Unit Price	Amount
TOTAL AMOUNT (IN WORDS)				

Ⅳ. Bill of Lading（提单）

		B/L NO. SEA GOLD TRANSPORTATION, INC. 金海国际航运有限公司 Combined Transport BILL of LADING
1 Shipper		RECEIVED in apparent good order and condition except as otherwise noted the total number of containers or other packages or units enumerated below for transportation hereof. One of the bills of lading must be surrendered duty endorsed in exchange for the goods or deliver order. On presentation of this document duly endorsed to the Carrier by or on behalf of the holder of the bill of lading, the rights and liabilities arising in accordance with the terms and conditions hereof shall, without prejudice to any rule of common law or statute rendering them binding on the Merchant, become binding in all respects between the Carrier and the Holder of the bill of lading as though the contract evidenced hereby had be made between them.
2 Consignee		
3 Notify Party		
4 Pre-carriage by	5 Place of Receipt	
6 Ocean Vessel Voy. No.	7 Port of Loading	
8 Port of Discharge	9 Place of Delivery	REFERENCE NO.

Marks & Nos. Container Seal No.	No. of containers or pkgs	Kind of Packages: Description of Goods	Gross Weight kgs	Measurement (CBM)
		Declared Cargo value USD _____ per Clause 5 on the reverse of this bill of lading. If Merchant enters a value. Carrier's per package limitation of liability shall not apply and the ad valorem rate in Carrier's tariff will be charged.		
10 TOTAL NO. OF CONTAINERS OR PACKAGES (IN WORDS)				

11 FREIGHT & CHARGES		Per	Prepaid	Collect	
EX. Rate:	Prepaid at		Payable at	Place and date of Issue	
	Total Prepaid		No. of Original B(s)/L	Signed for the Carrier	

V. Customs Declaration（报关单）

中华人民共和国海关进口货物报关单

预录入编号： 　　　　　　　　　　　　　海关编号：

进口口岸*		备案号		进口日期*		申报日期
经营单位		运输方式		运输工具名称		提运单号
收货单位*		贸易方式		征免性质		征税比例*
许可证号	起运国(地区)*		装货港*		境内目的地*	
批准文号	成交方式	运费		保费	杂费	
合同协议号	件数	包装种类		毛重(公斤①)	净重(公斤)	
集装箱号	随附单据				用途*	
标记唛码及备注						
项号 商品编号 商品名称规格型号 数量及单位 原产国(地区)* 单价 总价 币制 征免						
税费征收情况						
录入员 录入单位	兹声明以上申报无讹并承担法律责任			海关审单批注及放行日期(签章)		
报关员				审单 审价		
单位地址	申报单位(签章)			征税 统计		
邮编 电话	填制日期			查验 放行		

① 1公斤＝1 000克。

Ⅵ. Inspection of Goods（报检单）

中华人民共和国出入境检验检疫
入境货物报检单

报检单位（加盖公章）：　　　　　　　　　　编号_____
报检单位登记号：　　联系人：　　电话：　　报检日期：_____年___月___日
发 货 人　　　　　（中文）
　　　　　　　　　（外文）
收 货 人　　　　　（中文）
　　　　　　　　　（外文）
货物名称（中/外文）　H.S.编码　产地　数/重量　货物总值　包装种类及数量
运输工具名称号码　　　贸易方式　　　货物存放地点
合同号　　　　　　　信用证号　　　用　途
到货日期
启运地
集装箱规格、数量及号码
合同、信用证订立的　　标记及号码　　随附单据（划"V"或补填）
检验检疫条款或特殊要求

需要证单名称（划"V"或补填）　　　检验检疫费
品质证书　　植物检疫证书　　　总金额
重量证书　　　　　　　　　　　（人民币元）
兽医卫生证书
健康证书　　　　　　　　　计费人　领取证单
卫生证书　　　　　　　　　收费人　日期
动物卫生证书　　　　　　　　　　　签名
报检人郑重声明：
1 本人被授权报检。
2 上列填写内容正确属实，货物无伪造或冒用他人的厂名、标志、认证标志，并
　承担货物质量责任。
签名：_____

Ⅶ. Forwarding Order（托运委托书）

出 口 货 物 托 运 委 托 书

外运编号： 日期：		致：
出口托运单： SHIPPER：		
CONSIGNEE：		联系人：
NOTIFY PARTY：		日期：
PLACE OF RECEIPT：	PORT OF LOADING	电话：
PORT OF DISCHARGE：	PLACE OF DELIVERY	传真：
MARKS & NOS. NO. OF PACKAGES	DESCRIPTION OF GOODS G. W. (KGS)	MEAS.
运费支付方式	提单份数	可否分批(N/Y)	可否转运(N/Y)
提货地点	装运期	有效期	制单人

Ⅷ. Sales Contract（销售合同）

Sales Contract

合同编号：_____

Contract NO：_____

签订地点：_____

Signed at：_____

签订日期：_____

Date：_____

买方：_____

The Buyers：_____

卖方：_____

The Sellers：_____

双方同意按下列条款由买方买入、卖方售出下列商品：

The Buyers agree to buy and the Sellers agree to sell the following goods on terms and conditions as set forth below：

（1）商品名称、规格及包装

  Name of Commodity, Specifications and Packing

（2）数量

  Quantity

（3）单价

  Unit Price

（4）总值

  Total Value

  （装运数量允许有_____%的增减）

  (Shipment Quantity _____% more or less allowed)

（5）装运期限：_____
　　　Time of Shipment：_____

（6）装运口岸：_____
　　　Port of Loading：_____

（7）目的口岸：_____
　　　Port of Destination：_____

（8）保险：由_____方负责，按本合同总值110%投保_____险。
　　　Insurance：To be covered by the _____ for 110% of the invoice value against _____.

（9）付款：凭保兑的、不可撤销的、可转让的、可分割的即期有电报套汇条款/见票/出票_____天期付款信用证，信用证以_____为受益人并允许分批装运和转船。该信用证必须在_____前开到卖方，信用证的有效期应为上述装船期后第15天，在中国_____到期，否则卖方有权取消本售货合约，不另行通知，并保留因此而发生的一切损失的索赔权。

　　　Terms of Payment：By confirmed, irrevocable, transferable and divisible letter of credit in favour of _____ payable at sight with TT reimbursement clause/_____ days'/sight/date allowing partial shipment and transshipment. The covering Letter of Credit must reach the Sellers before _____ and is to remain valid in _____. China until the 15th day after the aforesaid time of shipment, failing which the Sellers reserve the right to cancel this Sales Contract without further notice and to claim from the Buyers for losses resulting therefrom.

（10）商品检验：以中国_____所签发的品质/数量/重量/包装/卫生检验合格证书作为卖方的交货依据。

Inspection: The Inspection Certificate of Quality / Quantity / Weight / Packing / Sanitation issued by _____ of China shall be regarded as evidence of the Sellers' delivery.

（11）装运唛头：_____

　　　　　Shipping Marks：_____

卖方（Sellers）：_____　　买方（Buyers）：_____

第二部分

金融篇

Unit 1 Daily Reception

🏃 Learning Objectives

1. Get to understand the importance of daily reception in the bank.
2. Try to master the useful notes and expressions on daily reception in the bank.
3. To learn how to make conversations when receiving customers in the bank.

🏃 Relative Information

Nowadays, domestic wealth in China has entered into a new stage of rapid growth. So people's demand for financial services is increasing gradually. Generally speaking, there are two mainly-used types of financial services: personal banking and business banking.

Take personal banking as an example. It consists of basic banking service, E-banking service, loans and mortgages, insurance and so on. Among them, the basic banking service has close relationship with people's daily life. Deposits and withdrawals, remittance, opening accounts, credit cards and other basic transactions all belong to it.

These transactions should be conducted at the corresponding counters. The person behind the counter is called the teller, who is responsible for the acceptance and payout of cash, issuing bank checks, accepting bill payments (e. g. electricity, gas, water, etc.), arranging money transfers between accounts, loss reporting, etc.

 Situational Dialogues

Dialogue One　Open an Account

Clerk: Welcome to Bank of China, Binhai Branch. What can I do for you?

Customer: Yes, please. I want to open an account, but I'm confused about the types of those accounts. Would you please introduce some to me?

Clerk: Of course. We usually provide current savings account and time savings account for individuals.

Customer: So what's the difference between them?

Clerk: The current account means that you can withdraw money anytime.

Customer: That's so convenient, but how about the interest rate?

Clerk: As far as the rate is concerned, if you open a time savings account, you'll get a certificate of deposit and enjoy a higher interest rate.

Customer: Thank you for the detailed information. If I just want to withdraw my salary in an account, which one should I choose to open?

Clerk: Do you need to withdraw money very frequently?

Customer: Yes, I use it to pay for my monthly housing mortgage.

Clerk: In that case, you'd better open a current account. You can withdraw money whenever you need.

Customer: That's OK. Would you please handle it for me?

Clerk: I'm so glad. Please show me your identity card and let me know how much you want to deposit, if you don't mind.

Customer: Here you are. My ID card and 50,000 yuan.

Clerk: Wait a moment please. Here's your ID card and deposit book.

Customer: Thank you for your kind service.

Clerk: It's very nice of you to choose our bank. I'm so glad to be of any assistance. Welcome to our bank again.

Dialogue Two   Deposit Some Money

Clerk: Good morning, Miss. Can I help you?

Customer: Yes. I'd like to make a time deposit.

Clerk: How much would you like to deposit?

Customer: 50,000 yuan. May I know the annual interest rate of time deposit?

Clerk: The bank can offer an interest rate of 2.25% per annum for the one-year time deposit.

Customer: Thank you. Here is the money. Please arrange it for me.

Clerk: All right. Would you like a passbook or a deposit certificate?

Customer: Passbook, please. Because I'd like to make time deposits regularly in the future years.

Clerk: OK. But would you please fill out this slip first? It's necessary if you'd like to deposit money. Please write down your name, account number, period and sum of your deposit, and then sign your name here.

Customer: (After filling out the form) Here you are.

Clerk: Thank you. Oh, I'm sorry to trouble you, but could you write the sum in words instead of in figures?

Customer: Oh, I'm sorry.

(The customer filled out a new form)

Clerk: It's correct this time. OK, everything is done, madam. Here is your passbook and the receipt. Please check it.

Customer: Thank you.

Dialogue Three   Report the Loss of a Card

Lobby Manager: Excuse me, sir. I'm the lobby manager. You look worried. Is there anything I can do for you?

Customer: Yes, thank you. My card was lost. Where can I report a loss?

Lobby Manager: I'm sorry to hear that. Come with me please. Your business will be conducted here. Don't worry.

Customer: Thanks. (Turn to the clerk)

Clerk: Is there anything I can do for you, Sir?

Customer: I've lost my Great Wall Card and I want to report the loss.

Clerk: Just take it easy. We will try our best to help you. May I ask when you lost it?

Customer: Yesterday afternoon. It is too late to report then. I'm afraid that my money has already been withdrawn by others.

Clerk: May I have your card number and name, as well as your passbook. I'll check whether your money is still on your account or not.

Customer: OK, here you are. My name's Tom Johnson and this is my card number.

Clerk: Mr. Johnson, would you please let me know how much money is in your card?

Customer: Yes. There is altogether 5,000 yuan.

Clerk: Wait a minute, please. (After a while) I'm so glad to tell you that your money hasn't been cashed. There's no withdrawal record since yesterday afternoon.

Customer: Great! Many thanks. But may I withdraw the balance immediately?

Clerk: I'm afraid not. Please fill in the Application Form of Loss Reporting detailedly. And then your fund will be blocked.

Customer: Does it mean nobody is able to withdraw my money if I conduct it?

Clerk: Sure. The next step is to fill out the application form to get a new card after three days. At that time, you can withdraw your money.

Customer: I see. Thank you.

Clerk: My pleasure.

Notes:

1. open an account 开立账户
2. current savings account 活期账户
3. time savings account 定期账户
4. interest rate 利率
5. housing mortgage 住房按揭
6. identity card 身份证
7. deposit book 存折
8. account number 账号
9. fill out 填写
10. report the loss 挂失
11. application form of loss reporting 挂失申请表

Important Sentences

1. What can I do for you?

2. We usually provide current savings account and time savings account for individuals.

3. You can withdraw money whenever you need.

4. Please show me your identity card and let me know how much you want to deposit, if you don't mind.

5. I'm so glad to be of any assistance.

6. The bank can offer an interest rate of 2.25% per annum.

7. But would you please fill out this slip first?

8. OK, everything is done, madam.

9. Excuse me, sir. I'm the lobby manager.

10. Is there anything I can do for you?

11. I've lost my Great Wall Card and I want to report the loss.

12. I'm afraid that maybe my money has already been withdrawn by others.

13. There's no withdrawal record since yesterday afternoon.

14. But may I withdraw the balance immediately?

15. And then your fund will be blocked.

 Tasks

1. Read this passage and translate it into Chinese

Nowadays, thousands of customers walk into banks conducting various financial businesses every day. Clerks in banks should first greet and receive customers warmly before providing specific services. When conducting specific businesses, they should communicate with and provide professional services to the customers with great patience and care.

2. Oral practice

A customer comes to the Chartered Bank to deposit some money. The clerk is required to help him open an account and explain the information about the difference between several types of account. Finally, the clerk conducts the deposit for the customer.

 Background Information

外国人在美国银行开立户头,需要携带护照或者驾驶执照等,只要能证明自己的身份即可。美国人开户时,往往是夫妻、姐妹或父子开共同户,否则一人遭遇不测或出远门时,其他家人就难以提款。

美国银行的活期存款分为储蓄存款、有利息支票存款、无利息支票存款等。普通存款可以每天存入或提出,利息低。开有利息支票户须在银行保持一定数额(例如底限1 000元)的存款,否则就不能开有利息支票户。开无利息支票户则通常有较低存款即可,有的银行会送支票,有的银行要客户自己买。银行会提供金融卡以方便客户存取款,信用卡的申请需建立个人信用后才有可能申请。

定期存款利息较高,但因留学生每学期或每月皆有固定支出,无法长期定存,所以不建议将钱放入定存。一般留学生会选择开支票账户及活期储蓄账户,两者并用。

开户所需证件如下:

(1) 护照

(2) ID Card 或驾驶执照

(3) 社会安全卡

Time for Relaxation

Job

Jack applied to a finance agency for a job, but he had no experience. He was so intense that the manager gave him a tough account with the promise that if he collected it, he'd get the job.

Two hours later, Jack came back with the entire account. "Amazing!" the manager said. "How did you do it?"

"Easy," Jack replied. "I told him if he didn't pay up, I'd tell all his creditors. He paid us."

Unit 2   Deposit and Withdrawal

Learning Objectives

1. Get to understand the procedures of deposit and withdrawal in the bank.
2. Try to master the useful notes and expressions on deposit and withdrawal in the bank.
3. To learn how to make conversations about deposit and withdrawal in the bank.

Relative Information

Maybe opening an account is the first step of establishing relations with the bank. Bank offers many different accounts to their customers. We mainly talk about two of them: current account and time account.

Current account, also called demand account, refers to an account that can be deposited and withdrawn at any time. Such account can also be set as payment account, from which the bank can make payments upon holder's requests. In current accounts, the bank doesn't need a withdrawal notice.

On the contrary, time account (fixed account) requires notice to the bank, usually seven days before the depositor has a right to make a withdrawal. Different maturities and amount of money deposited decide the interest rate. Naturally, the longer period of certificate you set, the higher interest rate you get.

Situational Dialogues

Dialogue One Deposit Money

Customer: Good morning, Miss. I'd like to deposit some money with your bank.

Clerk: Good morning. Thank you for choosing our bank.

Customer: May I ask about the interest rate?

Clerk: Please look at the electronic board which is now reflecting the different interest rates. And the rate varies with different maturities and different amount of money deposited. So how much and how long would you like to deposit?

Customer: I'd like to make a deposit of 5,000 yuan with one year term.

Clerk: I have noted it down. Maybe a fixed deposit would be your better choice.

Customer: Fixed deposit?

Clerk: It will offer you a higher interest, but the withdrawal time has to

be restricted according to the term chosen when opening the fixed account.

Customer: What if I need money urgently before the maturity date?

Clerk: It doesn't matter. You can withdraw your money at any time you like. But you can't receive the stated interest.

Customer: Would I lose all my interest if I withdraw in advance?

Clerk: No, not all. The interest rate will be calculated at the current deposit rate.

Customer: I see. Then how about forgetting to cash my money when the maturity comes?

Clerk: We'll just regard your account as a current one from then on.

Customer: OK. It would be better for me to choose a fixed account. I'm not in urgent need now.

Clerk: Please fill out the slip.

Customer: All right.

Dialogue Two Withdraw Money

Clerk: Is there anything I can do for you?

Customer: Yes, please. I would like to draw 1,000 dollars from my account.

Clerk: Please fill out this withdrawal slip.

Customer: My daughter hasn't got time to come with me. So would you please tell me how to fill in it?

Clerk: Of course. First of all, please take a form of this kind. Look at the title. Don't confuse it with deposit form. Then write down your name, the amount of money you want to draw and your passbook number in blanks.

Customer: I've got it. Please wait a few minutes.

Clerk: Can you see it clearly? There's a pair of presbyopic glasses available.

Customer: No, thanks. Which number should I write here, in words or in Arabic?

Clerk: You are required to write both in Chinese and in Arabic numbers. If you have any other problems, please come to ask me again.

Customer: Thank you for your kind help. (Several minutes later) I've finished filling in this form. Here it is.

Clerk: Please pass me your bankbook.

Customer: Here you are.

Clerk: Oh, your bankbook needs PIN.

Customer: What is PIN?

Clerk: That is your secret code.

Customer: My daughter has told me about it. (After entering the secret code) Is it all right?

Clerk: I'm sorry. The code number doesn't coincide with the one you used when you opened the account. Is it necessary to phone your daughter?

Customer: No, let me try it again. Is it correct this time?

Clerk: Yes. How would you like your money?

Customer: 500 dollars in one-hundred-dollar bills and then forty tens and twenty fives, please.

Clerk: Well, wait a moment. Here is your money, $1,000. Please check it and keep your bankbook carefully.

Customer: You've done me a great favor. Thank you for your patience.

Clerk: It was a real pleasure for me to do it.

Dialogue Three   Inquire about the Interest Rate

Clerk: Is there anything I can do for you, madam?

Customer: Yes. I would like to deposit some money. Could you please tell me the interest rate for a current account at present?

Clerk: Yes. It's 0.9%.

Customer: OK. How about the interest for the fixed deposit?

Clerk: For a one-year fixed deposit, we offer an interest rate of 3.25% per annum. And for three-year or five-year fixed ones, the interest rates will be higher.

Customer: The interest has fallen a lot, since it was 3.75% for a one-year fixed deposit three months ago, I remember. Then please arrange 5,000 yuan RMB deposit to my current account and here is my passbook.

Clerk: It's very convenient with a current account, we should say. Deposit or withdrawal can be made at any time. Please sign here, madam.

Customer: All right, here you are.

Clerk: Madam, everything is done. Here is your passbook. See you next time.

Customer: Thank you.

Notes:

1. current account/demand account 活期账户
2. time account /fixed account 定期账户
3. electronic board 电子显示板
4. maturity date 到期日
5. stated interest 原定的利息
6. be in urgent need 急需
7. coincide with 与……一致
8. bankbook/passbook 存折

Important Sentences

1. And the rate varies with different maturities and different amounts of money deposited.

2. I'd like to make a deposit of 5,000 yuan with one-year term.

3. What if I need money urgently before the maturity date?

4. Would I lose all my interest if I withdraw in advance?

5. I would like to draw 1,000 dollars from my account.

6. The code number doesn't coincide with the one you used when you opened the account.

7. You've done me a great favor.

8. Could you please tell me the interest rate for a current account at present?

9. For a one-year fixed deposit, we offer an interest rate of 3.25% per annum.

10. It's very convenient with a current account, we should say.

Tasks

1. Read this passage and translate it into Chinese

However, different accounts have different requirements in withdrawing money. For example, if you open a current savings account, also called demand account, you can withdraw money at any time when you need it. But if you open a time savings account, you can withdraw money only at the maturity of the account. Therefore, when a customer deposits or withdraws money in a bank, the clerk will first ask him what kind of account he is holding.

2. Oral practice

Imagine you're a customer who wants to deposit some money in ICBC. Your classmate is the clerk of this bank who offers his/her help. But you're not familiar with the types of account and don't know the procedure of deposit. During this conversation, you're required to talk about the types of account, the deposit amount, and the period of deposit if it's a fixed deposit.

Background Information

　　在美国，一般人付账无论金额大小，通常都是开支票或者刷卡，人们几乎不带现金或只带 10~20 美元的零钱，以备不时之需。开账户所需要的资料：两种证件，其中一种必须是带有照片的证件（护照、驾照、州身份证），另一种是不带照片的其他形式的证件（如信用卡、工作证或者学生证）；社会安全号码（如果有的话就提供，但有些银行并不需要）；100 美元的现金（学生 50 美元）。

　　存款业务是银行的传统业务。存款是存款人基于对银行的信任而将资金存入银行，并可以随时或按约定时间支取款项的一种信用行为。存款是银行对存款人的负债，是银行最主要的资金来源。

　　取款时一般不能透支，这是银行的规定。当你急需用钱时，取一些没到期的钱还是可以的，但是得不到原定的利息。但是如果不支取全部存款的话，剩下的钱还是会享有原来的利息的。

Time for Relaxation

Account

At a country-club party a young man was introduced to an attractive girl. Immediately he began to pay her court and flatter her outrageously. The girl liked the young man, but she was taken a bit aback by his fast and ardent pitch. She was amazed when 30 minutes later he seriously proposed marriage.

"Look," she said, "We only met half an hour ago. How can you be so sure? We know nothing about each other."

"You're wrong," the young man declared. "For the past five years, I've been working in the bank where your father has his account."

Unit 3 Remittance

 Learning Objectives

- Get to understand the procedure of remittance in the bank.
- Try to master the useful notes and expressions about remittance in the bank.
- To learn how to make conversations about remittance in the bank.

 Relative Information

Remittance refers to the process in which the remitter instructs the remitting bank to send the requested funds to a payee staying in places different from the remitter's. Remittance is part of a bank's international services and is divided into two categories: inward and outward.

Remittance mainly has three types: Telegraphic Transfer (T/T), Mail Transfer (M/T) and Banker's Demand Draft (D/D). In detail, T/T means that payment instruction is given by the remitting bank to the paying bank by means of telecommunication such as telegram, telex, or email, etc., while M/T by mail or courier in the form of Payment Order and in D/D, payment instruction is written down on the bank draft.

There is a key point in T/T and M/T that should be noted, i.e. the paying bank must authenticate whether the instruction received is really given by the remitting bank. After all, it is the paying bank that first pays to the payee and then claims for reimbursement from the remitting bank. In D/D, however, after receiving the draft issued by the remitting bank, the remitter may dispatch or even bring it to the payee in another place. Upon receipt of the draft, the payee will present it to the paying bank for payment.

 ## Situational Dialogues

Dialogue One Introduction to Remittance

Customer: Excuse me. Is this the remittance counter?

Clerk: Yes, madam. What can I do for you?

Customer: I'd like to remit some money to New York. But I'm not familiar with remittance. Would you please make a brief introduction to it?

Clerk: Certainly. Do you want to remit your money by T/T, M/T or D/D?

Customer: What are the meanings of these abbreviations?

Clerk: They are short for Telegraphic Transfer, Mail Transfer and Banker's Demand Draft, respectively.

Customer: Could you please explain them in details?

Clerk: Of course, madam. T/T is actually a cipher telegram sent by the remitting bank to the foreign receiving bank, instructing the receiving bank to pay a certain amount of money to the beneficiary.

Customer: So it's supposed to be faster than M/T.

Clerk: Yes, T/T is the quickest but the commission is the highest.

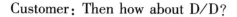

Customer: Then how about D/D?

Clerk: D/D is another mode of remittance which is often used when you go abroad. Before you start the journey to a foreign country, you can apply for D/D, which means a domestic bank draws a sight bill on its foreign correspondent bank.

Customer: Is it convenient for me to cash the bill?

Clerk: Yes. You can take the sight bill out with you and go to the designated receiving bank to have it cashed.

Customer: It must be safer than carrying money abroad. Thank you for your introduction, which is very professional. Then I know how to choose a proper mode of remittance according to the specific situation.

Clerk: I'm very glad to be of some assistance. After you choose the suitable mode of remittance, you're required to fill in the Application for Remittance.

Customer: What's that?

Clerk: Please look at this form. (Show it to the customer) You need to write down the names and addresses of both the remitter and the beneficiary, and the sum to be remitted.

Customer: OK. I completely make clear now. Thank you.

Clerk: Not at all.

Dialogue Two Inward Remittance

Clerk: Good afternoon. Welcome to the Industrial and Commercial Bank of China. May I help you?

Customer: Good afternoon. May I ask where an inward remittance is handled?

Clerk: Right here, Sir.

Customer: I'd like to check whether $1,000 remitting from Los Angeles has arrived.

Clerk: I'll check it for you. But may I have your name first?

Customer: Henry Hill.

Clerk: Mr. Hill, do you have a foreign currency current account with our bank?

Customer: Yes, I have.

Clerk: Wait a moment, please. I'm sorry, but your remittance hasn't arrived yet.

Customer: Really? My daughter made the remittance one day ago. It should have arrived. So what's the matter with it?

Clerk: Generally speaking, if the money was sent by cable, it would take about one or two days, while it would take at least one week by air mail.

Customer: My daughter has told me that the money had been sent by cable.

Clerk: Maybe your money will arrive tomorrow.

Customer: I hope so.

Clerk: Do you mind telling me your telephone number? We will contact you if your remittance arrives.

Customer: You're so considerate. This is my business card.

Clerk: Please rest assured. I'll phone you the minute your remittance arrives.

Customer: I don't know how I can thank you enough.

Clerk: Glad to have been of help. Hope to see you again.

Dialogue Three Outward Remittance

Clerk: What can I do for you, sir?

Customer: I want to remit some money to New York. Is it handled here?

Clerk: Yes, sir. What currency do you want to remit?

Customer: US dollar.

Clerk: OK. How much would you like to remit?

Customer: What I have here is 210,000 yuan RMB. I want to change it into US dollar and then send it to New York.

Clerk: Would you mind telling me the reason for the remittance?

Customer: My sister is in an urgent need of the money for her education.

Clerk: I see. But you know, we have rather strict foreign exchange control regulations, and anybody who wants to exchange the Renminbi yuan for the foreign currency must get approval from the Foreign Exchange Control Bureau. You have to present us a license for conversion and outgoing remittance.

Customer: Oh, I've got the relevant documents…Here you are.

Clerk: OK, thank you … The current rate is seven yuan for one dollar. Then 210,000 yuan RMB can be exchanged into 30,000 yuan RMB. By the way, how would you like to remit your money? I suggest a telegraphic transfer.

Customer: Yeah, that's exactly what I want. T/T goes relatively faster.

Clerk: OK, sir. Now please fill in this application form for remittance… Besides, we will charge you 0.1% as service commission and the cable charge is 150 yuan.

Customer: OK, please deduct directly from this card.

Notes:

1. telegraphic transfer (T/T) 电汇
2. mail transfer (M/T) 信汇

3. banker's demand draft (D/D) 票汇

4. upon receipt of 一收到

5. remitting bank 汇出行

6. sight bill 即期票据,见票即付票据

7. by cable/ by air mail 用电报发出,通过电报/用航空邮件

8. foreign currency 外币,外汇

9. Foreign Exchange Control Bureau 外汇管理局

10. service commission 服务费

Important Sentences

1. T/T is actually a cipher telegram sent by the remitting bank to the foreign receiving bank, instructing the receiving bank to pay a certain amount of money to the beneficiary.

2. You can take the sight bill out with you and go to the designated receiving bank to have it cashed.

3. You need to write down the names and addresses of both the remitter and the beneficiary, and the sum to be remitted in it.

4. I'd like to check whether $1,000 remitting from Los Angeles has arrived.

5. Mr. Hill, do you have a foreign currency current account with our bank?

6. Do you mind telling me your telephone number?

7. Is it handled here?

8. What currency do you want to remit?

9. You have to present us a license for conversion and outgoing remittance.

10. The current rate is seven yuan for one dollar.

Tasks

1. Read this passage and translate it into Chinese

A telegraphic transfer is an instruction from the importer's bank to the exporter's bank or his branch in the exporter's country to transfer some of the balance in its account to the person named in the transfer. The importer pays his bank the local currency equivalent of the sum in foreign currency that the correspondent bank hands over to the exporter. Telegraphic transfer is by far the most rapid and convenient way for a remitter to send a sum to the beneficiary when the latter is in urgent need of the funds. There is little risk that a T/T has been delayed or has failed to reach its destination, but the remittance charge is rather expensive. The bank's charge for the transfer will be either paid by the importer or the exporter.

2. Oral practice

Imagine you want to remit some money to Paris. Your sister lives there and she is now in urgent need of a large sum of money. You're hesitated to choose the proper way of your remittance. With the help of bank clerk, you are finally successful in remitting.

 Background Information

在国外，好朋友或家人之间可能彼此会有对方的客户资料，这样就可以把钱存进彼此的账户里。这是一种方便的转账方法。不过把账户资料转给别人时要小心，有时候朋友甚至家人也会受到金钱的诱惑。开支票转账比较安全，但是实效性和速度可能差了一点儿，因为支票要几天后才能结清，意思是说必须等到银行授权才能拿到钱。汇票是由银行所开的支票，它也是一种转账方法。银行会担保钱一定拿得到。汇票可以立即兑现，但是手续费较高，而且客户要在银行营业时间内亲自跑一趟银行才可以办成。

Time for Relaxation

Real US Dollars

Not long after an old Korean woman came back to Korea from her visit to her daughter in the states, she went to a city bank to deposit the US dollars her daughter gave her. At the bank counter, the clerk checked each note carefully to see if the money was real. It made the old lady out of patience.

At last she could not hold any more, uttering, "Trust me, Sir, and trust the money. They are real US dollars. They are directly from America."

Unit 4　Loans and Credit Cards

Learning Objectives

1. Get to understand the procedure of applying for loans and credit cards in the bank.
2. Try to master the useful notes and expressions on applying for loans and credit cards in the bank.
3. To learn how to make conversations when applying for loans and credit cards in the bank.

Relative Information

Banks grant a wide range of loans to customers for different purposes. Bank loans can be divided into the following main categories.

Real estate loans, which are secured by real property such as land and buildings, etc., include short-term loans for real estate developers to develop land and conduct buildings and long-term loans for individuals or companies to purchase personal apartments or commercial buildings.

Commercial loans, which are secured by business companies, are mainly employed in purchasing raw materials, assembly lines, advanced techniques, and paying salaries, etc.

Loans to individuals, which are secured by individuals for personal purposes, are mainly used in purchasing automobiles, household appliances and many other commodities, repairing and decorating houses, and paying for medical care.

To some extent, credit card is a kind of loan extended to individuals by the bank to buy various kinds of commodities and services. The issuer of the card grants its user a certain line of credit within which the user can borrow money for payment to merchants or as cash advance.

Situational Dialogues

Dialogue One Housing Loan

Customer: Good morning. Is this the Credit and Loan Department?

Clerk: Yes, sir. I'm the manager of Credit and Loan Department. This is my business card.

Customer: Nice to meet you, Mr. Wang.

Clerk: Nice to meet you too. Is there anything I can do for you?

Customer: Yes, please. I want to buy a new house and I'd like to inquire about the housing loan offered by your bank.

Clerk: I'm very pleased to be of some help. Generally speaking, our bank mainly provides two types of housing loans: mortgage loan and accumulation fund loan.

Customer: What's the difference between them?

Clerk: Let me introduce in detail. If you have an accumulation fund account in our bank and have made successive deposits into this account for over six months, you're qualified to apply for the personal housing loan on the accumulation fund. And more importantly, the interest rate is lower than mortgage loan.

Customer: I see. But it's a pity that I haven't got such an account and I can't wait to buy the house right now.

Clerk: Then you'd better apply for mortgage loan, which can also be called commercial loan.

Customer: Well. How much and how long can I borrow from your bank?

Clerk: It depends. I wonder whether it's your first house. If so, you're required to pay down payment of 30% of the whole according to the regulations. If it's the second one, then 50% will be OK. We can finance you with the rest of your purchase price.

Customer: That seems good. How long is the maturity for a loan?

Clerk: Long tenor available up to 30 years and short tenor upon your request.

Customer: What supporting materials should I provide?

Clerk: You need present us with your ID card, income certificate, marital status certificate, formal house purchase contact and other related documents.

Customer: I see.

Clerk: Here is the service guide for personal housing loan for your reference.

Customer: Thank you very much.

Dialogue Two Foreign Currency Loan

Clerk: Good morning. This is International Business Department of

ICBC Tianjin Branch. Can I help you?

Customer: I am from ABC Import and Export Company. Could you supply us with a foreign currency loan?

Clerk: Yes, of course. But we must make an investigation of your credit standing, the operational state of your enterprise, your repayment capability and so on.

Customer: I see. This is a detailed report about our financial status and credit standing.

Clerk: We'll pay immediate attention to your report and tell you our decision in a week or so.

Customer: Thanks a lot. By the way, would you please explain the terms and the interest rate of the foreign currency loan respectively?

Clerk: We have short-term, mid-term and long-term loans, fixed or floating rate loans with security or without.

Customer: Then I'd like a loan for 2 years at a fixed rate with security.

Clerk: What currency and how much do you want?

Customer: For three million US Dollars.

Clerk: Then we will specify a loan program according to your condition and we will tell you our decision within 2 weeks.

Customer: Thank you. Contact me as soon as possible and it's convenient at any time.

Dialogue Three　Credit Card

Customer: Good morning, I'm thinking of having a credit card. Would you please tell me something about it?

Clerk: Sure, my pleasure. In brief, you can purchase first and pay later.

Customer: Is that true?

Clerk: Certainly, you can use credit card to pay for daily expenditure instead of carrying much cash, and you can pay back the fund one month later.

Customer: But what should I do if I lost my credit card? Is it possible for someone else to consume and charge the purchase to my account?

Clerk: Definitely not. Each credit card has its own secret code. When you lose your card, you should report to us without any delay. We'll cancel your card immediately.

Customer: Sounds great. Your prompt response to it makes it safer and more convenient.

Clerk: You're right. Nowadays almost every department store, hotel, supermarket, restaurant offer the installment payment for credit card users.

Customer: That's great. How can I apply for a credit card?

Clerk: Would you please present your identity card first?

Customer: Yes, here you are.

Clerk: Thank you. Besides, we need some details of your personal creditworthiness, such as your monthly salary and other professional income. Of course all the information is kept strictly confidential.

Customer: Oh, I'm now in the field of high technology, which provides me with a fixed monthly salary of about 6,000 yuan RMB.

Clerk: Your stable income qualifies you for the application of a credit card.

Customer: And then?

Clerk: You just have to fill in this form and offer it to us with a copy of your salary statement, ID card and passbook records of your major accounts for the last three months.

Customer: One more thing, what determines the credit limit of the card?

Clerk: Your salary and credit rating do.

Customer: Apart from these, does your bank offer a credit card bonus points programme?

Clerk: Certainly. Actually you'll accumulate points for getting a prize each time you use it.

Customer: Great. How long can I get my credit card?

Clerk: It will take one week to issue and post the credit card after we check all your documents.

Customer: Thank you for introduction.

Clerk: It's the least I could do for you.

Notes:

1. credit and loan department 信贷部
2. housing loan 住房贷款
3. mortgage loan 按揭贷款
4. accumulation fund loan 公积金贷款
5. be qualified to 具有……的资格
6. down payment 首期付款
7. income certificate 收入证明
8. marital status certificate 婚姻状况证明
9. credit standing 信用状况
10. floating rate 浮动利率
11. credit card bonus points 信用卡积分

Important Sentences

1. I'm very pleased to be of some help.
2. But it's a pity that I haven't got such an account and I can't wait to buy the house right now.
3. We can finance you with the rest of your purchase price.
4. Long tenor available up to 30 years and short tenor upon your request.
5. I am from ABC Import and Export Company.

6. What currency and how much do you want?

7. Then we will specify a loan program according to your condition and we will tell you our decision within 2 weeks.

8. We'll cancel your card immediately.

9. Your stable income qualifies you for the application of a credit card.

10. You just have to fill in this form and offer it to us with a copy of your salary statement, ID card and passbook records of your major accounts for the last three months.

 Tasks

1. Read this passage and translate it into Chinese

When you are considering buying a new apartment with the help of the mortgage loan extended by the bank, make sure that you are clear in mind. How is the interest counted? Take a 30-year repayment schedule as an example. On a 30-year term, 150,000 yuan mortgage with a fixed interest rate of 7.5 percent, a homeowner who keeps the loan for the full term will pay 227,575 yuan in interest. The lender can't possibly expect that person to pay all that interest in just a couple of years so the interest is spread over the full 30-year term. That keeps the monthly payment at 1,048 yuan.

2. Oral practice

Imagine you're the clerk working in the Credit and Loan Department. The customer wants to apply for a loan from the bank to buy a new car. But he knows little about loans, and you need to offer help to the customer.

 Background Information

在加拿大,要使用信用卡,最好的办法就是保持低透支限额,然后每个月都全额还清欠款。这样可以避免支付利息和罚款。客户必须清楚每个月可以负担得起多少金额,然后把那个金额设为限额。要告诉信用卡公司，不要调高你的透支限额。

　　房屋抵押贷款是一种只能用来买房子的特殊贷款。当银行把钱贷给客户购置房产时，便称为房屋抵押贷款。客户每年可以额外还款一次。那笔款项会直接还掉本金而不是用来还利息。这样可以让抵押贷款早点还清。有些人会每个月存一些钱来付这笔重要的额外款项，以便早日拥有自己的房子并还清负债。

Time for Relaxation

Do You Take Children?

　　When a man called a motel and asked how much they charged for a room, the clerk told him that the rates depend on the room size and the number of people.

　　"Do you take children?" the man asked.

　　"No, Sir," replied the clerk. "Only cash and credit cards."

Unit 5　E-banking

Learning Objectives

1. Get to know the wide usage of E-banking.
2. Try to master the useful notes and expressions on the business of E-banking.
3. To learn how to make conversations when conducting business through E-banking.

Relative Information

E-banking provides customers with a virtual platform. A customer can serve himself through Internet, telephone or mobile phone. Thus, e-banking can be divided into three main categories: Internet banking, telephone banking and mobile banking. Enterprises, institutions and individuals can log on a bank's website, dial a service number or send short messages to conduct e-banking services, such as making inquiries, wealth management, remittance transfer and settlement, etc.

Nowadays, with the rapid rhythm of people's lives and the increasing requirements of various kinds of people, e-banking has already become one of the necessary aids of modern people. E-banking eliminates physical and geographic boundaries and time limitations of banking services. Compared with traditional banking services, labor is replaced by machine, which is low in cost and competitive in efficiency. As a result, it is believed that e-banking can help banks to achieve the objectives of higher customer acceptance and satisfaction, higher profitability and enhanced competitive advantages. E-banking period is coming.

Situational Dialogues

Dialogue One Internet Banking

Customer: I'd like to apply for Personal Internet Banking.

Clerk: If you want an online self-service bank, you should open an account with our bank.

Customer: I've already had an account with your bank, and also a credit card.

Clerk: You just fill out the application form against your personal valid certificates and credit card.

Customer: Would you please tell me what financial services the Personal Internet Banking can provide?

Clerk: My pleasure. Account transfer, account management fee paying agency, remittance, etc. all belong to Personal Internet Banking. In a word, you can do all these by yourself on your computer.

Customer: It sounds more convenient to manage my account than before and it can save much time.

Clerk: Yes, it can satisfy different financial needs of our customers.

Customer: But how to ensure the security of the personal Internet Banking?

Clerk: You should set an entry password which is different from the one you withdraw money. The system will also instruct you to download the security controls. Furthermore, USB shield can also be applied for to protect the security of your account.

Customer: Great! If I want to remit, how do you charge?

Clerk: The service charge is 1%, the floor is 1 yuan and the ceiling is 50 yuan.

Customer: OK. Thank you for the information. I'll apply for one.

Clerk: OK, I'll transact for you right away.

Dialogue Two　Telephone Banking

Customer: Excuse me, I wonder if I can check my account balance by phone instead of going to the counter?

Clerk: Of course, Sir. You're just required to apply for the phone banking service for your account.

Customer: Wonderful. But would you please show me how to apply for it?

Clerk: It's very easy to sign up for the phone banking service. Here is the booklet for phone banking service which includes all the services. Please take and read it carefully.

Customer: OK. It must be of some help.

Clerk: It's really easy to do and you won't have to come into the bank as usual.

Customer: That would be very convenient. But how much should I pay for signing up the phone banking service?

Clerk: The personal telephone banking is free of charge currently.

Customer: Great! How to operate? According to the booklet given by you, I just need call the phone banking number, and then enter the relevant services according to what I hear.

Clerk: Yes, it's incredibly easy. You should call 95588 at first and you'll hear the voice prompts, just follow the instructions.

Customer: OK. If I want to check my balance, how should I do?

Clerk: After you hear the voice, you may press the No. 1 button.

Customer: And then?

Clerk: Then input your account number or your ID card number, ending with the # button. After that you should enter the secret code. It's very necessary and crucial, which can secure the safety of your account.

Customer: Yes, secret code can avoid certain loss of the customer's account. Otherwise, choosing telephone banking service would be very dangerous. So is that all?

Clerk: Yes, you can choose such functions as inquiry of account balance, funds transfer, and renewal of secret code...by pressing 1,2,3,...

Customer: It's a little difficult for the person of my age?

Clerk: Don't worry. You can refer to the booklet of operation I've given.

Customer: Oh, yes. It can save a lot of trouble.

Clerk: If there's something difficult for you to deal with by yourself, you can ask for my help.

Customer: Thank you very much.

Clerk: It's my pleasure.

Dialogue Three   Mobile Phone Banking

Clerk: How can I help you?

Customer: Yes, please. I'd like to know something about the mobile banking introduced by your bank recently.

Clerk: OK. You can apply for mobile banking through Internet or at our business offices.

Customer: Why is it so well-received? Would you please tell me the most attractive advantage it has?

Clerk: To put it simple, the mobile banking can be used as your pocket coagent.

Customer: Sounds interesting. What does it mean?

Clerk: It can include almost any kind of financial management, such as inquiry, remittance, transfer, consumption, payment of charges, etc. It's so convenient that you can even conduct the above businesses by sending short messages.

Customer: It's just like a mini ATM. But how can I register my own mobile banking?

Clerk: The most important thing is that your mobile phone is web-enabled.

Customer: Yes, and then?

Clerk: Then you must have an account with our bank.

Customer: OK, I have one.

Clerk: That's good. I'll handle it for you.

Customer: Thank you.

(Ten minutes later)

Clerk: That's OK. Your mobile banking is opened now.

Customer: It maybe a little difficult for a beginner to operate.

Clerk: Don't worry. Just follow the indications and all the functions have an indication menu in both Chinese and English.

Customer: How about the charges as you know?

Clerk: Registering for telephone banking is free of charge. And 0.10 yuan for sending each short message. The telephone bill is the same as a local call rate if you need other business by phoning.

Customer: It's so nice.

Clerk: Yes, it can make our life more efficient.

Customer: Definitely, thank you!

Clerk: All my pleasure.

Notes:

1. apply for 申请
2. personal valid certification 个人有效证件
3. account transfer 转账
4. security control 安全控件
5. USB shield U盾
6. according to 按照
7. voice prompt 语音提示
8. secret code 密码
9. pocket coagent 随身携带的好帮手
10. indication menu 提示菜单

Important Sentences

1. If you want an online self-service bank, you should open an account with our bank.

2. You just fill out the application form against your personal valid certificates and credit card.

3. Account transfer, account management fee paying agency, remittance, etc. all belong to Personal Internet Banking.

4. How to ensure the security of the personal Internet Banking?

5. The system will also instruct you to download the security controls.

6. Would you please show me how to apply for it?

7. It's very easy to sign up for the phone banking service.

8. How much should I pay for signing up the phone banking service?

9. The personal telephone banking is free of charge currently.

10. You should call 95588 at first and you'll hear the voice prompts, just follow the instructions.

11. Then input your account number or your ID card number, ending with the # button.

12. If there's something difficult for you to deal with by yourself, you can ask for my help.

13. I'd like to know something about the mobile banking introduced by your bank recently.

14. Would you please tell me the most attractive advantage it has?

15. It's so convenient that you can even conduct the above businesses by sending short messages.

16. The most important thing is that your mobile phone is web-enabled.

17. Just follow the indications which have Chinese and English menu.

18. Registering for telephone banking is free of charge.

 Tasks

1. Read this passage and translate it into Chinese

Electronic Banking allows customers to conduct financial transactions, for example: monthly salary inquiry, cash deposit and withdrawal, funds transfer, account balance checking, consumption, payment of charges and other banking services. The feature is that people can obtain certain financial businesses without going to the banks directly.

2. Oral practice

A lady wants to inquire about her monthly salary and bonus. The clerk suggests that she open the telephone banking and shows her how to operate.

 Background Information

网上银行最早起源于美国,其后迅速蔓延到 Internet 所覆盖的各个国家。美国安全第一网络银行(SFNB)从 1996 年就开始了网上金融服务,美国银行业 6%~7% 的客户使用网上银行系统。

目前,国际上提供网上银行服务的机构分两种:一种是原有的负担银行(incumbent bank),机构密集,人员众多,在提供传统银行服务的同时推出网上银行系统,形成营业网点、ATM、POS 机、电话银行、网上银行的综合服务体系;另外一种是信息时代崛起的直接银行(direct bank),机构少,人员精,采用电话、Internet 等高科技服务手段与客户建立密切的联系,提供全方位的金融服务。

 Time for Relaxation

A Good Boy

Little Peter asked his mother for two cents.

Mum: "What did you do with the money I gave you yesterday?"

Peter: "I gave it to a poor old woman."

Mum: "You're a good boy, here are two cents more. But why are you so kind? The old lady must be moved! Mum is so proud of you!"

Peter: "Thank you, mum. She is the one who sells the ice-cream."

Appendix

 Ⅰ.世界各国(或地区)的货币名称及符号大全

Different Currencies of the World

亚洲		货币名称		货币符号		辅币进位制
		中文	英文	原有旧符号	标准符号	
中国	香港	港元	Hong Kong Dollars	HK $	HKD	1HKD = 100 cents(分)
	澳门	澳门元	Macao Pataca	PAT.;P.	MOP	1MOP = 100 avos(分)
	内地	人民币元	Renminbi yuan	RMB ¥	CNY	1CNY = 10 jiao(角) 1 jiao = 10 fen(分)

续表

亚洲	货币名称		货币符号		辅币进位制
	中文	英文	原有旧符号	标准符号	
朝鲜	朝鲜圆	Korean Won		KPW	1KPW = 100 分
越南	越南盾	Vietnamese Dong	D.	VND	1VND = 10 角 = 100 分
日本	日圆	Japanese Yen	¥;J.¥	JPY	1JPY = 100 sen(钱)
老挝	老挝基普	Laotian Kip	K.	LAK	1LAK = 100 ats(阿特)
柬埔寨	柬埔寨瑞尔	Camboddian Riel	CR. ;J Ri.	KHR	1KHR = 100 sen(仙)
菲律宾	菲律宾比索	Philippine Peso	Ph. Pes. ; Phil. P.	PHP	1PHP = 100 centavos(分)
马来西亚	马元	Malaysian Dollar	M. $; Mal. $	MYR	1MYR = 100 cents(分)
新加坡	新加坡元	Singapore Dollar	S. $	SGD	1SGD = 100 cents(分)
泰国	泰铢	Thai Baht (Thai Tical)	BT. ;Tc.	THP	1THP = 100 satang(萨当)
缅甸	缅元	Burmese Kyat	K.	BUK	1BUK = 100 pyas(分)
斯里兰卡	斯里兰卡卢比	Sri Lanka Rupee	S. Re. 复数;S. Rs.	LKR	1LKR = 100 cents(分)
马尔代夫	马尔代夫卢比	Maldives Rupee	M. R. R; MAL. Rs.	MVR	1MVR = 100 larees(拉雷)

续表

亚洲	货币名称		货币符号		辅币进位制
	中文	英文	原有旧符号	标准符号	
印度尼西亚	印度尼西亚盾	Indonesian Rupiah	Rps.	IDR	1IDR = 100 cents（分）
巴基斯坦	巴基斯坦卢比	Pakistan Rupee	Pak. Re.；P. Re. 复数：P. Rs.	PRK	1PRK = 100 paisa（派萨）
印度	印度卢比	Indian Rupee	Re. 复数：Rs.	INR	1INR = 100 paise（派士）（单数：paisa）
尼泊尔	尼泊尔卢比	Nepalese Rupee	N. Re. 复数：N. Rs.	NPR	1NPR = 100 paise（派司）
阿富汗	阿富汗尼	Afghani	Af.	AFA	1AFA = 100 puls（普尔）
伊朗	伊朗里亚尔	Iranian Rial	RI.	IRR	1Irr = 100 dinars（第纳尔）
伊拉克	伊拉克第纳尔	Iraqi Dinar	ID	IQD	1IQD = 1,000 fils（费尔）
叙利亚	叙利亚镑	Syrian Pound	£.Syr.；£.	SYP	1SYP = 100 piastres（皮阿斯特）
黎巴嫩	黎巴嫩镑	Lebanese Pound	£ L.	LBP	1LBP = 100 piastres（皮阿斯特）
约旦	约旦第纳尔	Jordanian Dinar	J. D.；J. Dr.	JOD	1JOD = 1,000 fils（费尔）

续表

亚洲	货币名称		货币符号		辅币进位制
	中文	英文	原有旧符号	标准符号	
沙特阿拉伯	沙特阿拉伯亚尔	Saudi Arabian Riyal	S. A. Rls. ; S. R.	SAR	1SAR = 100 qurush（库尔什） 1qurush = 5 halals（哈拉）
科威特	科威特第纳尔	Kuwaiti Dinar	K. D.	KWD	1KWD = 1,000 fils（费尔）
巴林	巴林第纳尔	Bahrain Dinar	BD.	BHD	1BHD = 1,000 fils（费尔）
卡塔尔	卡塔尔里亚尔	Qatar Riyal	QR.	QAR	1QAR = 100 dirhams（迪拉姆）
阿曼	阿曼里亚尔	Oman Riyal	RO.	OMR	1OMR = 1,000 baiza（派沙）
阿拉伯也门	也门里亚尔	Yemeni Riyal	YRL.	YER	1 YER = 100 fils（费尔）
民主也门	也门第纳尔	Yemeni Dinar	YD.	YDD	1YDD = 1,000 fils（费尔）
土耳其	土耳其镑	Turkish Pound (Turkish Lira)	£ T. (TL.)	TRL	1TRL = 100 kurus（库鲁）
塞浦路斯	塞浦路斯镑	Cyprus Pound	£ C.	CYP	1CYP = 1,000 mils（米尔）

续表

大洋洲	货币名称		货币符号		辅币进位制
	中文	英文	原有旧符号	标准符号	
澳大利亚	澳大利亚元	Australian Dollar	$ A.	AUD	1AUD = 100 cents（分）
新西兰	新西兰元	New Zealand Dollar	$ NZ.	NZD	1NZD = 100 cents（分）
斐济	斐济元	Fiji Dollar	F. $	FJD	1FJD = 100 cents（分）
所罗门群岛	所罗门元	Solomon Dollar.	SL. $	SBD	1SBD = 100 cents（分）

欧洲	货币名称		货币符号		辅币进位制
	中文	英文	原有旧符号	标准符号	
欧洲货币联盟	欧元	Euro	EUR	EUR	1EUR = 100 euro cents（生丁）
冰岛	冰岛克朗 复数：Kronur	Icelandic Krona	I. Kr.	ISK	1ISK = 100 aurar（奥拉）
丹麦	丹麦克朗 复数：Kronur	Danish Krona	D. Kr.	DKK	1DKK = 100 ore（欧尔）

续表

大洋洲	货币名称		货币符号		辅币进位制
	中文	英文	原有旧符号	标准符号	
挪威	挪威克朗	Norwegian Krone 复数:Kronur	N. Kr.	NOK	1NOK = 100 ore(欧尔)
瑞典	瑞典克朗	Swedish Krona 复数:Kronur	S. Kr.	SEK	1SEK = 100 ore(欧尔)
芬兰	芬兰马克	Finnish Markka (or Mark)	MK.;FM.; FK.;FMK.	FIM	1FIM = 100 penni(盆尼)
俄罗斯	卢布	Russian Ruble or Rouble	Rbs.;Rbl.	SUR	1SUR = 100 kopee(戈比)
波兰	波兹罗提	Polish Zloty	ZL.	PLZ	1PLZ = 100 groszy(格罗希)
捷克和斯洛伐克	捷克克朗	Czechish Kronur	Kcs.; Cz. Kr.	CSK	1 CSK = 100 Hellers = (赫勒)
匈牙利	匈牙利福林	Hungarian Forint	FT.	HUF	1HUF = 100 filler(菲勒)
德国	德国马克	Deutsche Mark	DM.	DEM	1DEM = 100 fennig(芬尼)
奥地利	奥地利先令	Austrian Schilling	Sch.	ATS	1ATS = 100 = Groschen (格罗申)

续表

大洋洲	货币名称		货币符号		辅币进位制
	中文	英文	原有旧符号	标准符号	
瑞士	瑞士法郎	Swiss Franc	SF. ;SFR.	CHF	1CHF = 100 centimes(分)
荷兰	荷兰盾	Dutch Guilder (or Florin)	Gs. ;Fl. ; Dfl. ; Hfl. ;fl.	NLG	1NLG = 100 cents(分)
比利时	比利时法郎	Belgian Franc	Bi. ; B. Fr. ; B. Fc.	BEF	1BEF = 100 centimes(分)
卢森堡	卢森堡法郎	Luxembourg Franc	Lux. F.	LUF	1LUF = 100 centimes(分)
英国	英镑	Pound, Sterling	£ ;£ Stg.	GBP	1GBP = 100 new pence(新便士)
爱尔兰	爱尔兰镑	Irish pound	£ . Ir.	IEP	1IEP = 100 new pence(新便士)
法国	法国法郎	French Franc	F. F. ;Fr. Fc. ; F. FR.	FRF	1FRF = 100 centimes(分)
西班牙	西班牙比塞塔	Spanish Peseta	Pts. ;Pes.	ESP	1ESP = 100 centimos(分)
葡萄牙	葡萄牙埃斯库多	Portuguese Escudo	ESC.	PTE	1PTE = 100 centavos(分)
意大利	意大利里拉	Italian Lira	Lit.	ITL	1ITL = 100 centesimi(分)

续表

大洋洲	货币名称		货币符号		辅币进位制
	中文	英文	原有旧符号	标准符号	
马耳他	马耳他镑	Maltess Pound	£．M．	MTP	1MTP = 100 cents（分） 1cent = 10 mils（米尔）
南斯拉夫	南斯拉夫新第纳尔	Yugoslav Din	Din．Dr．	YUD	1YUD = 100 paras（帕拉）
罗马尼亚	罗马尼亚列伊复数：Leva	Rumanian Leu	L．	ROL	1ROL = 100 bani（巴尼）
保加利亚	保加利亚列弗复数：Lei	Bulgarian Lev	Lev．	BGL	1BGL = 100 stotinki（斯托丁基）
阿尔巴尼亚	阿尔巴尼亚列克	Albanian Lek	Af．	ALL	1ALL = 100 quintars（昆塔）
希腊	希腊德拉马克	Greek Drachma	Dr．	GRD	1GRD = 100 lepton（雷普顿）or lepta（雷普塔）

美洲	货币名称		货币符号		辅币进位制
	中文	英文	原有旧符号	标准符号	
加拿大	加元	Canadian Dollar	Can．$	CAD	1CAD = 100 cents（分）
美国	美元	U．S．Dollar	U．S．$	USD	1USD = 100 cent（分）

续表

美洲	货币名称		货币符号		辅币进位制
	中文	英文	原有旧符号	标准符号	
墨西哥	墨西哥比索	Mexican Peso	Mex. $	MXP	1MXP = 100 centavos（分）
危地马拉	危地马拉格查尔	Quatemalan Quetzal	Q	GTQ	1GTQ = 100 centavos（分）
萨尔瓦多	萨尔瓦多科朗	Salvadoran Colon	¢	SVC	1SVC = 100 centavos（分）
洪都拉斯	洪都拉斯伦皮拉	Honduran Lempira	L.	HNL	1HNL = 100 centavos（分）
尼加拉瓜	尼加拉瓜科多巴	Nicaraguan Cordoba	CS	NIC	1NIC = 100 centavos（分）
哥斯达黎加	哥斯达黎加科朗	Costa Rican Colon	¢	CRC	1CRC = 100 centavos（分）
巴拿马	巴拿马巴波亚	Panamanian Balboa	B.	PAB	1PAB = 100 centesimos（分）
古巴	古巴比索	Cuban Peso	Cu. Pes.	CUP	1CUP = 100 centavos（分）
巴哈马联邦	巴哈马元	Bahaman Dollar	B. $	BSD	1BSD = 100 cents（分）
牙买加	牙买加元	Jamaican Dollars	$.J.	JMD	1JMD = 100 cents（分）

续表

美洲	货币名称		货币符号		辅币进位制
	中文	英文	原有旧符号	标准符号	
海地	海地古德	Haitian Gourde	G. ;Gds.	HTG	1HTG = 100 centimes（分）
多米尼加	多米尼加比索	Dominican Peso	R. D. $	DOP	1DOP = 100 centavos（分）
特立尼达和多巴哥	特立尼达和多巴哥元	Trinidad and Tobago Dollar	T. T. $	TTD	1TTD = 100 cents（分）
巴巴多斯	巴巴多斯元	Barbados Dollar	BDS. $	BBD	1BBD = 100 cents（分）
哥伦比亚	哥伦比亚比索	Colombian Peso	Col $	COP	1COP = 100 centavos（分）
委内瑞拉	委内瑞拉博利瓦	Venezuelan Bolivar	B	VEB	1VEB = 100 centimos（分）
圭亚那	圭亚那元	Guyanan Dollar	G. $	GYD	1GYD = 100 cents（分）
苏里南	苏里南盾	Surinam Florin	S. Fl.	SRG	苏 1SRG = 100 分

续表

美洲	货币名称		货币符号		辅币进位制
	中文	英文	原有旧符号	标准符号	
秘鲁	秘鲁新索尔	Peruvian Sol	S/.	PES	1PES = 100 centavos（分）
厄瓜多尔	厄瓜多尔苏克雷	Ecuadoran Sucre	S/.	ECS	1ECS = 100 centavos（分）
巴西	巴西新克鲁赛罗	Brazilian New Cruzeiro G	Gr. $	BRC	1BRC = 100 centavos（分）
玻利维亚	玻利维亚比索	Bolivian Peso	Bol. P.	BOP	1BOP = 100 centavos（分）
智利	智利比索	Chilean Peso	P.	CLP	1CLP = 100 centesimos（分）
阿根廷	阿根廷比索	Argentine Peso	Arg. P.	ARP	1ARP = 100 centavos（分）
巴拉圭	巴拉圭瓜拉尼	Paraguayan Guarani	Guars.	PYG	1PYG = 100 centimes（分）
乌拉圭	乌拉圭新比索	New Uruguayan Peso	N. $	UYP	1UYP = 100 centesimos（分）

续表

非洲	货币名称		货币符号		辅币进位制
	中文	英文	原有旧符号	标准符号	
埃及	埃及镑	Egyptian Pound	£ E. ;LF.	EGP	1EGP = 100 piastres(皮阿斯特) = 1,000 milliemes(米利姆)
利比亚	利比亚第纳尔	Libyan Dinar	LD.	LYD	1LYD = 100 piastres(皮阿斯特) = 1,000 milliemes(米利姆)
苏丹	苏丹镑	Sudanese Pound	£ S.	SDP	1SDP = 100 piastres(皮阿斯特) = 1,000 milliemes(米利姆)
突尼斯	突尼斯第纳尔	Tunisian Dinar	TD.	TND	1TND = 1,000 milliemes(米利姆)
阿尔及利亚	阿尔及利亚第纳尔	Algerian Dinar	AD.	DZD	1DZD = 100 centimes(分)
摩洛哥	摩洛哥迪拉姆	Moroccan Dirham	DH.	MAD	1MAD = 100 centimes(分)
毛里塔尼亚	毛里塔尼亚乌吉亚	Mauritania Ouguiya	UM	MRO	1MRO = 5 khoums(库姆斯)
塞内加尔	非共体法郎	African Financial Community Franc	C. F. A. F.	XOF	1XOF = 100 centimes(分)
上沃尔特	非共体法郎	African Financial Community Franc	C. F. A. F.	XOF	1XOF = 100 centimes(分)

续表

非洲	货币名称		货币符号		辅币进位制
	中文	英文	原有旧符号	标准符号	
科特迪瓦	非共体法郎	African Financial Community Franc	C. F. A. F.	XOF	1XOF = 100 centimes（分）
多哥	非共体法郎	African Financial Community Franc	C. F. A. F.	XOF	1XOF = 100 centimes（分）
贝宁	非共体法郎	African Financial Community Franc	C. F. A. F.	XOF	1XOF = 100 centimes（分）
尼泊尔	非共体法郎	African Financial Community Franc	C. F. A. F.	XOF	1XOF = 100 centimes（分）
冈比亚	冈比亚达拉西	Gambian Dalasi	D. G.	GMD	1GMD = 100 bututses（分）
几内亚比绍	几内亚比索	Guine-Bissau peso	PG.	GWP	1GWP = 100 centavos（分）
几内亚	几内亚西里	Guinean Syli	GS.	GNS	辅币为科里 cauri，但50科里以下舍掉不表示；50科里以上进为一西里。
塞拉利昂	利昂	Sierra Leone Leone	Le.	SLL	1SLL = 100 cents（分）

续表

非洲	货币名称		货币符号		辅币进位制
	中文	英文	原有旧符号	标准符号	
利比里亚	利比里亚元	Liberian Dollar	L.＄£;Lib.＄	LRD	1LRD = 100 cents（分）
加纳	加纳塞地	Ghanaian Cedi	¢	GHC	1GHC = 100 pesewas（比塞瓦）
尼日利亚	尼日利亚奈拉	Nigerian Naira	N	NGN	1NGN = 100 kobo（考包）
喀麦隆	中非金融合作法郎	Central African Finan-Coop Franc	CFAF	XAF	1XAF = 100 centimes（分）
乍得	中非金融合作法郎	Central African Finan-Coop Franc	CFAF	XAF	1XAF = 100 centimes（分）
刚果	中非金融合作法郎	Central African Finan-Coop Franc	CFAF	XAF	1XAF = 100 centimes（分）
加蓬	中非金融合作法郎	Central Africa Finan-Coop Franc	CFAF	XAF	1XAF = 100 centimes（分）
中非	中非金融合作法郎	Central African Finan-Coop Franc	CFAF	XAF	1XAF = 100 centimes（分）

续表

非洲	货币名称		货币符号		辅币进位制
	中文	英文	原有旧符号	标准符号	
赤道几内亚	赤道几内亚埃奎勒	Equatorial Guinea Ekuele	EK.	GQE	1GQE = 100 centimes（分）
南非	兰特	South African Rand	R.	ZAR	1ZAR = 100 cents（分）
吉布提	吉布提法郎	Djibouti Franc	DJ. FS；DF	DJF	1DJF = 100 centimes（分）
索马里	索马里先令	Somali Shilling	Sh. So.	SOS	1SOS = 100 cents（分）
肯尼亚	肯尼亚先令	Kenya Shilling	K. Sh	KES	1KES = 100 cents（分）
乌干达	乌干达先令	Uganda Shilling	U. Sh.	UGS	1UGS = 100 cents（分）
坦桑尼亚	坦桑尼亚先令	Tanzania Shilling	T. Sh.	TZS	1TZS = 100 cents（分）
卢旺达	卢旺达法郎	Rwanda Franc	RF.	RWF	1RWF = 100 cents（分）
布隆迪	布隆迪法郎	Burnudi Franc	F. Bu	BIF	1BIF = 100 cents（分）
扎伊尔	扎伊尔	Zaire Rp Zaire	Z.	ZRZ	1ZRZ = 100 makuta（马库塔）

续表

非洲	货币名称		货币符号		辅币进位制
	中文	英文	原有旧符号	标准符号	
赞比亚	赞比亚克瓦查	Zambian Kwacha	KW.；K.	ZMK	1ZMK = 100 nywee（恩韦）
马达加斯加	马达加斯加法郎	Franc de Madagasca	F. Mg.	MCF	1MCF = 100 cents（分）
塞舌尔	塞舌尔卢比	Seychelles Rupee	S. RP（S）	SCR	1SCR = 100 cent（分）
毛里求斯	毛里求斯卢比	Mauritius Rupee	Maur. Rp.	MUR	1MUR = 100 centimes（分）
津巴布韦	津巴布韦元	Zimbabwe Dollar	ZIM. $	ZWD	1ZWD = 100 cents（分）
科摩罗	科摩罗法郎	Comoros Franc	Com. F.	KMF	1KMF = 100 tambala（坦巴拉）

Ⅱ. 精选货币及票面赏析

Appreciation of Currencies and Denomination

美元

英镑

欧元

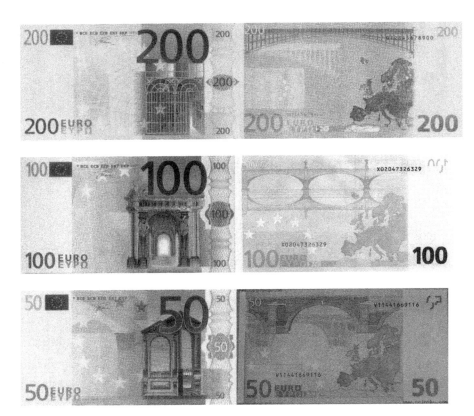

加元

日元

新西兰元

澳元

港币

卢布

Ⅲ. 中国主要银行名称及标志

Names and Logos of Major Banks in China

中文名称	英文名称	标志
中国银行	Bank of China(BOC)	中国银行 BANK OF CHINA
中国人民银行	The People's Bank of China(PBC)	中国人民银行 THE PEOPLE'S BANK OF CHINA
中国建设银行	China Construction Bank(CCB)	中国建设银行 China Construction Bank
中国工商银行	Industrial and Commercial Bank of China(ICBC)	中国工商银行

续表

中文名称	英文名称	标志
中国农业银行	Agricultural Bank of China(ABC)	
中国邮政储蓄银行	Postal Savings Bank of China	
中国进出口银行	Export-import Bank of China	
中国农业发展银行	Agricultural Development Bank of China(ADBC)	
国家开发银行	China Development Bank(CDB)	
交通银行	Bank of Communications	
招商银行	China Merchants Bank	
中国光大银行	China Everbright Bank	
上海浦东发展银行	Shanghai Pudong Development Bank	
平安银行	Ping An Bank Co., Ltd.	
广东发展银行	Development Bank of Guangdong	

续表

中文名称	英文名称	标志
中国民生银行	China Minsheng Banking Corp., Ltd.	
兴业银行	Industrial Bank Co., Ltd	
中信银行	China CITIC Bank	
北京银行	Bank of Beijing	
华夏银行	Huaxia Bank	
渤海银行	China Bohai Bank	
浙商银行	China Zheshang Bank	
恒丰银行	Evergrowing Bank	
杭州银行	Bank of Hangzhou	
杭州联合银行	Hangzhou United Bank	

Ⅳ. 世界各国主要银行一览

☆ 英国
- 阿比国民银行 Abbey National
- 巴克莱银行 Barclays Bank PLC.
- 劳埃德银行 Lloyds Bank PLC.
- 米兰银行 Midland Bank
- 国民西敏寺银行 National Westminster Bank PLC.

☆ 法国
- 巴黎国民银行 Banque Nationale de Paris
- 里昂信贷银行 Credit Lyonnais
- 太平洋安全银行 de Caisse Nationale Credit Agricole

☆ 巴西
- 巴西银行 Banco Do Brasil

☆ 日本
- 第一劝业银行 Dai-Ichi Kangyo Bank
- 东海银行 Tokai Bank
- 东京银行 Bank of Tokyo
- 富士银行 Fuji Bank
- 大和银行 Daiwa Bank
- 日本兴业银行 Industrial Bank of Japan
- 三和银行 Sanwa Bank
- 三井银行 Mitsui Bank
- 三菱银行 Mitsubishi Bank
- 住友信托银行 Sumitomo Trust & Banking

☆ 美国
- 第一洲际银行 First Interstate Bancorp
- 大通曼哈顿银行 Chase Manhattan Bank

- 花旗银行 Citibank
- 梅隆国民银行 Mellon National Corp.
- 摩根保证信托银行 Morgan Guaranty Trust Corp. of New York
- 纽约化学银行 Chemical New York Corp.
- 纽约银行家信托公司 Bankers Trust New York Corp.
- 芝加哥第一国民银行 First Chicago Corp.

☆ 德国
- 德累斯顿银行 Dresdner Bank
- 德意志银行 Deutsche Bank
- 西德意志地方银行 Westdeutsche Landesbank Girozentrale

☆ 荷兰
- 荷兰通用银行 Algemene Bank Nederland

☆ 瑞士
- 瑞士信贷银行 Credit Suisse
- 瑞士银行公司 Swiss Bank Corp
- 瑞士联合银行 Union Bank of Switzerland

☆ 加拿大
- 加拿大皇家银行 Royal Bank of Canada
- 多伦多自治领银行 Toronto-Dominion Bank
- 加拿大帝国商业银行 Canadian Imperial Bank of Commerce

☆ 意大利
- 都灵圣保罗银行 Istituto Bancario SanPaolo Di Torino
- 国民劳动银行 Banca Nazionale del Lavor
- 伦巴省储蓄银行 Cassa Di Risparmio Delle Provincie Lombarde
- 西亚那银行 Monte Dei Paschi Di Siena
- 意大利商业银行 Banca Commerciale Italiana
- 意大利信贷银行 Credito Italiano

☆ 荷兰
- 荷兰农业合作社中央银行 Cooperatieve Centrale Raifferssen
- 汉华实业银行 Boerenleen Bank

☆ 中国香港
- 汇丰银行 Hong Kong and Shanghai Banking Corp. 香港
- 香港东亚银行 Bank of East Asia(BEA)

☆ 澳大利亚
- 西太平洋银行公司 Westpac Banking Corp.

参 考 文 献

[1] 袁俊娥,马永富. 翻开就会说的商务英语口语[M]. 北京:中国宇航出版社,2009.

[2] 李硕. 商务英语口语万言书[M]. 大连:大连理工大学出版社,2010.

[3] 王正元. 商务贸易英语口语[M]. 大连:大连理工大学出版社,2011.

[4] 张丽丽. 商务英语口语一定要速成[M]. 大连:大连理工大学出版社,2011.

[5] 牛淑敏,杨海燕. 商贸口语[M]. 大连:大连理工大学出版社,2012.

[6] 陈晶晶. 外贸英语口语脱口而出[M]. 北京:机械工业出版社,2011.

[7] 程祥麟. 银行柜面英语会话[M]. 南京:译林出版社,2008.

[8] 陈晶晶,等. 金融英语口语脱口而出[M]. 北京:机械工业出版社,2012.

[9] 姜建清. 银行业务英语学习[M]. 北京:中国金融出版社,2009.

[10] [加拿大]C·阿尼森. 实战银行英语会话[M]. 南京:译林出版社,2009.

[11] 汪卫芳,徐冯璐. 银行临柜英语[M]. 杭州:浙江大学出版社,2013.

[12] 沈素萍. 金融英语阅读教程[M]. 北京:中国金融出版社,2000.